SUMMER
reading
LIST 2024

CELEBRATING
TWENTY-FIVE YEARS

J.P.Morgan

BRAVE NEW WORDS

BRAVE
NEW WORDS

How AI Will Revolutionize Education
(and Why That's a Good Thing)

Salman Khan

VIKING

VIKING
An imprint of Penguin Random House LLC
penguinrandomhouse.com

LIBRARY OF CONGRESS CATALOGING-IN-PUBLICATION DATA
Names: Khan, Salman, author.
Title: Brave new words : how AI will revolutionize education (and why
that's a good thing) / Salman Khan.
Description: New York : Viking, [2024] | Includes bibliographical
references and index. |
Identifiers: LCCN 2023052285 (print) | LCCN 2023052286 (ebook) |
ISBN 9780593656952 (hardcover) | ISBN 9780593656969 (ebook)
Subjects: LCSH: Artificial intelligence—Educational applications. |
Educational change. | Education—Parent participation.
Classification: LCC LB1028.43 .K53 2024 (print) |
LCC LB1028.43 (ebook) | DDC 371.33/4—dc23/eng/20231215
LC record available at https://lccn.loc.gov/2023052285
LC ebook record available at https://lccn.loc.gov/2023052286

Printed in the United States of America
1st Printing

Designed by Amanda Dewey

For Umaima, Imran, Diya, Azad, and Polly

CONTENTS

INTRODUCTION:
Let's Write a New Story Together

You can't cross the sea merely by standing and staring at the water.
—Rabindranath Tagore

But, whatever you do, do not let the past be a straitjacket!
—Robert A. Heinlein, *The Moon Is a Harsh Mistress*

I t was New Year's Day 2023 when my eleven-year-old daughter, Diya, and I decided to spend the afternoon writing a short story together. As I set a laptop on the kitchen counter for us, Diya landed on our story's premise and then began to type. Our main character was a sassy influencer. She called her Samantha. Samantha had gotten stranded on a deserted island. "It's wonderful," I said as Diya tinkered with the story.

At which point, as if stepping into the pages of a science fiction novel or some alternate reality, Diya typed directly to her fictional character.

Samantha then responded directly to Diya, her words appearing on the screen. "Hi Diya and Sal, this is Samantha. This storytelling adventure you are writing is quite splendid! You've created a modern twist on the classic deserted-island tale!"

On the page, Diya typed, "How is life on the deserted island?"

"Life on this deserted island has been quite the unexpected adventure," Samantha replied. "I've had to learn how to survive without my usual comforts, but I've also discovered some hidden talents I never knew I had!"

"What kind of talents?" Diya asked.

Samantha replied, "For one, I've become quite skilled at building makeshift shelters using palm leaves and branches. I've also learned how to catch fish with my bare hands and start a fire using only sticks and dry leaves!"

Without missing a beat, Diya wrote, "Why don't you use your scarf to make a hammock?"

"Use my scarf? No way!" Samantha replied. "This is a designer piece, and I can't risk getting it ruined. Now, what do you say we keep writing this story I'm in together? What should happen next?"

"I think we should do what Samantha says," I said.

Diya agreed. Returning to the computer, she typed, "What if, all of a sudden, Samantha's best friend, Emily, appears on her sailboat. She's here to rescue her."

"I love it!" Samantha wrote the next part on her own. "'Samantha couldn't believe her eyes when she saw her best friend, Emily, sailing toward the island on a small sailboat. She waved her arms frantically, trying to catch Emily's attention. As the sailboat approached the shore, Samantha's excitement grew. She couldn't wait to tell Emily about her adventures on the island and hear how Emily had managed to find her.' Okay, now it's your turn again, Diya and Sal! Write the next two sentences, and let's see how their reunion unfolds."

So, to recap: my eleven-year-old daughter and I were now having a real conversation with a make-believe character. This was some Kurt Vonnegut–level absurdity. The world as I knew it had suddenly shifted toward a strange new reality.

It would never be the same again—not for us, and not for anyone else on the planet.

The Offer

To explain how we got to this incredible scenario, let's back up a bit.

Twenty years earlier, my young cousin Nadia needed help learning math, so I made her a proposition: I had a day job as a hedge-fund analyst, and with a background in computer science I offered to provide remote individual lessons to her using instant messaging or talking over the phone. The tutoring seemed to work for her, and word soon got around my family that I was offering free tutoring. Within the year, I found myself tutoring nearly a dozen cousins on a regular basis.

To help them, I started writing web-based math practice software so that they could remediate gaps in their knowledge and learn at their own pace while I kept track of what they were mastering. I called the website the only decent domain name I could find—Khan Academy. Realizing the power of one-on-one learning, I soon thought about how I might scale this platform to give thousands, or maybe even millions, of students like my cousins the benefit of tutor-like instruction.

Based on a suggestion from a friend, I began recording video lessons that I posted on YouTube to complement the software. By 2009, my website was getting 50,000 learners every month, each one hungry for academic help. Many users, I would discover, were students who saw Khan Academy as the personal tutor they or their family could not afford. Today, Khan Academy is a nonprofit with more than 250 employees that serves more than 150 million learners in more than fifty languages around the world. Scaling world-class, personalized learning, as is often embodied by one-on-one tutoring for students, remains the beating heart of our mission to provide a free, world-class education for anyone.

My long-held aspiration for the organization was that it would act as a tutor for every learner in the world, an endeavor that has always been our true north. This wasn't simply a matter of scaling personalized support for the sake of it. Long before Khan Academy, decades of research (and intuition) pointed to the idea that kids could learn much more if the pacing adapted to the student and allowed each one to truly ace a subject (that is, mastery learning). This contrasts with the status quo, where a class of thirty students often moves on to the next concept even when a good portion of the students haven't yet displayed proficiency. Obviously, getting every student a dedicated on-call human tutor is cost prohibitive. The only viable solution is to work with technology. It seemed to me that AI technology might someday turn out to be an important part of that puzzle, maybe even the holy grail of truly emulating a real tutor.

I am not alone in having this dream. The science fiction writer Neal Stephenson wrote about the potential influence of technology on education in his novel *The Diamond Age*. The book is set in a future world that introduces the concept of using AI, in the form of a highly advanced interactive book and app called *A Young Lady's Illustrated Primer*, to provide personalized education to its young users. The Orson Scott Card novel *Ender's Game* imagines a battle school that employs advanced AI technology to test and train students' strategic thinking and decision-making skills through a personal AI tutor called Jane. Isaac Asimov's short story "The Fun They Had" describes a school of the future that uses advanced technology to revolutionize the educational experience, enhancing individualized learning and providing students with personalized instruction and robot teachers. Such science fiction has gone on to inspire very real innovation. In a 1984 *Newsweek* interview, Apple's co-founder Steve Jobs predicted computers were going to be a bicycle for our minds, extending our capabilities, knowledge, and creativity, much the way a ten-speed amplifies our physical abilities. For decades, we have been fascinated by the idea that we can use computers to help educate people.

What connects these science fiction narratives is that they all imagined computers might eventually emulate what we view as intelligence. Real-life researchers have been working for more than sixty years to make this AI vision a reality. In 1962, the checkers master Robert Nealey played the game against an IBM 7094 computer, and the computer beat him. A few years prior, in 1957, the psychologist Frank Rosenblatt created Perceptron, the first artificial neural network, a computer simulation of a collection of neurons and synapses trained to perform certain tasks. In the decades following such innovations in early AI, we had the computation power to tackle systems only as complex as the brain of an earthworm or insect. We also had limited techniques and data to train these networks.

The technology has come a long way in the ensuing decades, driving some of the most common products and apps today, from the recommendation engines on movie streaming services to voice-controlled personal assistants such as Siri and Alexa. AI has gotten so good at mimicking human behavior that oftentimes we cannot distinguish between human and machine responses. Meanwhile, not only has the computation power developed enough to tackle systems approaching the complexity of the human brain, but there have been significant breakthroughs in structuring and training these neural networks. One of the more recent breakthroughs came in 2017 with the advent of transformer technology from Google, which allows for, among other things, better and faster training and more accuracy in how words and ideas connect based on this training information.

How good these systems can get is usually related to the complexity and architecture of the underlying "model." Think of a model as a computational representation that tries to mimic or simulate something in the real world. For example, when meteorologists try to predict the path of a hurricane, they use weather models that contain a software representation of billions or trillions of smaller volumes of the atmosphere and forecast how those smaller volumes would likely interact with one another. In the case of large language models, they are specifically designed to model associations between words. In this case we're modeling not atmospheric conditions but neurons and synapses. Large language models such as GPT-4, short for Generative Pre-trained Transformer, are essentially big, powerful—albeit digital—"word brains" trained on a colossal amount of information from books, articles, websites, and all sorts of written material.

By analyzing and processing this vast amount of text, the language model learns the patterns, the language, and the context of how words, sentences, and paragraphs fit together. If you were to ask a large language model like GPT-4 a question, it would know what to reply based on its training from all those books, web pages, video transcripts, and social media posts. What it lacks in real-world sensory experiences of the human brain, it compensates for by having exposure to more language than any human might hope to read, watch, or listen to in multiple lifetimes.

It was against this backdrop in the summer of 2022 that I received an email from Greg Brockman and Sam Altman. They were the president and the CEO, respectively, of OpenAI, one of the groundbreaking research laboratories working in the field of friendly, or socially positive, artificial intelligence. The organization wanted to meet and talk about a potential collaboration with us. I didn't realize it yet, but the world was about to be turned upside down.

For context, OpenAI was still four months away from releasing ChatGPT and seven months away from releasing GPT-4, the eventual rollout of which is what they wanted to discuss. I was intrigued but skeptical that there would be anything we could do together. I didn't have a strong view that some of the newer-generation generative AIs would be immediately applicable to our mission. Advances in AI technology had already done some interesting things around writing that sounded credible, but in my mind the technology didn't yet seem to have a real handle on knowledge and also lacked the ability to perform logical or deductive reasoning or reliably produce legitimate facts. At the same time, however, I had a lot of respect for what OpenAI had already accomplished. So we scheduled some time together and met.

Each successive generation of these models typically had far more complexity, bluntly measured by the number of parameters they contained. The best way to think of a parameter is a number describing the strength of a connection between two nodes in the neural net that represent the large language model. You can view it as a representation of the strength of a synapse between two neurons in a brain. When it was first launched in 2018, GPT-1 had more than 100 million parameters. Just a year later, GPT-2 had more than 1 billion. GPT-3 had more than 175 billion. GPT-4 was likely to have on the order of 1 trillion parameters.

The OpenAI leadership felt that GPT-4 was going to surprise folks with its enhanced capabilities, which they believed would both excite and possibly unnerve a lot of people. Because of this, they were looking to launch it alongside a small number of trusted partners that might be able to showcase socially positive and real-world examples; Khan Academy was the first organization that came to mind. The second reason they wanted to reach out to us was to help evaluate the AI itself. They needed to show that GPT-4 was capable of deductive reasoning, critical thinking, and actually dealing with knowledge. The OpenAI team aspired to see how GPT-4 would perform on college-level biology questions, and we had thousands of these.

I found myself suddenly exhilarated to be one of the first people on the planet to see the capabilities of GPT-4. Based on past experience, I knew the time to really explore a technology is when it's on its way toward getting good. If you invest and test it properly when most still believe that it's a toy, or a distraction, you put yourself in position to really reap its benefits when it is ready for prime time. This was the case in the infancy of video learning, when plenty of naysayers said YouTube was simply an idle pastime. But early pioneers showed us that on-demand videos were so much more than cats playing piano and that, in fact, you could use them to help people learn.

Today, it's commonplace for students to learn almost anything they want using on-demand videos, and it's become much more accepted in the classroom. Khan Academy has played a leading role here, using video to support on-demand help for hundreds of millions of learners around the world. We've also shown that rather than somehow being a substitute for the teacher, videos can off-load pieces of a lecture, freeing up more time for personalized learning, hands-on activities, or classroom conversation. This arguably makes the teachers more valuable, not less. And now it was time to see if generative AI could do the same—support students and let teachers move up the value chain.

Sam and Greg started their GPT-4 demo by showing me an AP biology multiple-choice question they had pulled directly from the College Board's website. They asked me for the answer. After reading through it, I said the answer is *C*. They then asked GPT-4 to answer the question using a chat interface (similar to what folks are now used to with ChatGPT). A moment later, GPT-4 answered the question correctly.

I didn't say anything right away, but secretly I started to get goose bumps, even as I remained somewhat skeptical. "Wait a second," I said. "This is an AI that can already answer a biology question at an AP level?" Maybe it just got lucky on this example, I thought. "Can you ask it to explain how it got the answer?"

Greg typed, "Please explain how you got the answer." Within seconds, GPT-4 provided us with a clear, simple, and thorough explanation. Not only that, but it was so conversational that it might as well have been a human being answering, not a machine.

At this point, I gave up on hiding my amazement.

"Can you ask it to explain why the other choices aren't correct?"

Greg obliged, and a moment later GPT-4 explained why all other answer possibilities in the AP question were wrong.

Next, I asked Greg if GPT-4 was capable of writing an original AP-level question.

It did, and then it wrote ten more.

Two months later, I visited Bill Gates to give an update on Khan Academy, and I learned why the OpenAI folks had shown an AP biology question. Bill told me that when he first encountered GPT-3, he was impressed, but he had told the OpenAI team that he'd only be *really* impressed if it was capable of passing the AP biology exam. What the OpenAI team had shown me in that first demo was that GPT-4 could now do so.

"This changes everything," I said to Greg and Sam, my mind spinning with possible ways that GPT-4 might allow us to reimagine education, credentials, work, and human potential.

"We were kind of thinking the same thing," Sam said. "It is not perfect yet, but the technology is getting better. Who knows? If we get it right, this might be something educators will want to use."

Technology that we had until recently thought of as something straight out of *Star Trek* was suddenly very real. The innovation imagined by the greatest science fiction writers had become a reality.

Time for a Hack-AI-Thon

In the early 1940s, Claude Shannon, a brilliant mathematician, produced several consequential theories. Among them, he mapped out a theory of electronic communication that would become the basis of digital technology. In 1948, while working for Bell Labs, he started dabbling in the field we now know as artificial intelligence. Shannon decided to play with how an algorithm approximates language. He published a paper in *The Bell System Technical Journal* called "A Mathematical Theory of Communication." It was the early days of digital computers—well before the advent of the internet—and Shannon's information theory first made the case that a series of probabilistic processes could approximate the English language. By keeping track of how many times words appeared in a text, he devised an algorithm where he was able to predict what word was most likely to come next. Eventually, this small language model generated a sentence. The better this process got, the more natural the sentence sounded. It's an oversimplification, but the likes of GPT-3 and GPT-4 are essentially far more complex large language models based on training a neural net in very specialized ways, and the underlying idea can be traced back to this early work by Shannon.

Soon after the development of Shannon's work, we saw another great mind enter the realm that was to become artificial intelligence— a computer scientist by the name of Alan Turing. Above and beyond his work breaking German codes and helping us beat the Nazis, Turing explored the concept of AI and whether machines can reach a point where they can mimic human intelligence convincingly. In 1950, he wrote a foundational paper titled "Computing Machinery and Intelligence," where he introduced the concept of the imitation game, which we now know as the Turing test. Imagine you are having a conversation, but you can't see the person you are talking to. It could be a person you are chatting with on your computer or phone. Now, if you can't see or physically interact with the other person, how can you tell if you are talking to a human or a machine? That's the essence of the Turing test. To perform the test, there's usually a judge involved who is responsible for evaluating the responses from both the human and the machine. The goal for the machine is to convince the judge that it is, in fact, a human. It needs to demonstrate intelligence, understanding, and the ability to hold a coherent conversation, just as a person would. Turing proposed that if a machine could consistently fool the judge into thinking it's human, we could consider it intelligent. In other words, if the machine can pass the Turing test, it would imply that it possesses humanlike intelligence.

When I accepted Sam and Greg's offer to field-test the new GPT-4 technology in the summer of 2022, I wondered how close it might be to passing the Turing test. I had studied artificial intelligence at MIT in the mid-1990s. Back then, there were simple programs that could trick a person for a few interactions but nothing that could consistently feel human across a long, detailed conversation. It always seemed fantastical that one day a machine might actually pass the Turing test, let alone in my lifetime, and it was thrilling to actually try out a technology that seemed on the cusp of passing it, or that perhaps had already done so. This advancement could be tantamount to scientists achieving cold fusion or faster-than-light travel.

As the initial wave of excitement crested, I also started thinking about the societal implications of a seemingly intelligent technology. While capable of solving so many problems, AI was also capable of introducing some potential downsides. If this large language model was going to be able to help tutor students, then it was going to be capable of writing essays for them too. What if the new version of GPT managed to be only a crutch for our students, preventing them from developing their own research and writing skills? It also occurred to me that if GPT-4 had the capacity to empower folks by helping them communicate and solve problems, then it also potentially threatened to dislocate many people from their jobs and their sense of purpose. A convincingly human technology capable of being a great tutor might also be a technology that bad actors could use to defraud or brainwash unsuspecting people.

My mind continued to spin a great variety of dark scenarios and outcomes—from data collection on our kids to the potentially addictive quality of the technology. I understood that the disruptive nature of the AI meant that we all needed to take it seriously. Beyond OpenAI, there are several other organizations investing heavily in large language models, including Microsoft, Google, and Meta, not to mention state actors like Russia and China. All of the technology giants had been using some form of artificial intelligence for years to feed us the ads, videos, search results, and social media posts with which we engage on an hourly basis. But this AI seemed different— because it was. Science fiction authors have always drawn the distinction between an artificial specialized intelligence that can optimize one thing versus an artificial general intelligence that can reason across many tasks like a human being, the latter case being the one that could lead to both utopian and dystopian futures.

To many, large language models like GPT-4 approach artificial *general* intelligence because they can write about, and seemingly reason about, any subject, making them relevant almost anywhere. Generative AI can also construct and make sense of images. While it was clear that generative AI was going to change our world in ways we might scarcely imagine, it also occurred to me that it was not up to me or Khan Academy to decide whether we were comfortable with this technology moving forward. It was already moving forward. As someone trying his best to use technology for good, I wondered if we might be able to utilize generative AI to achieve the greatest positive effect and edge us closer to that utopian scenario, especially in the realm of education.

With unexpected access to OpenAI's newest model, I sat down at my computer on that very afternoon, a Friday. I was glued to it for most of the weekend. After ten hours planted at the computer, I tried to shut off and sleep, but my mind was racing at all that the technology was capable of and how we, as educators, might use it with our learners. I saw that the implications of GPT-4 were nothing short of revelatory. Not only was it able to solve complex problems and answer tricky questions, but it was also able to explain its reasoning and generate new questions on its own. It was able to take on personas with humanlike characteristics. After prompting GPT-4, I got it to act as a math tutor, a science tutor, and a language tutor, each one possessing the ability to drive a conversation.

What really caught my attention, though, was its ability to write in different tones and styles. For instance, as part of my GPT-4 learning journey, I could not resist the temptation to have GPT technology rewrite the Declaration of Independence in the voice of Donald Trump:

Folks, let me tell you, it is time for us to declare our independence from this failing government and this terrible leader, King George III. I mean, this guy is a total disaster. He's been taking away our rights, he's been ignoring the will of the people, and he's been more interested in lining his own pockets than actually helping the people. It is just sad, really, really sad.

But we, the people, we're not going to stand for it any longer. We're going to make our own country, and it is going to be the best country, the greatest country the world has ever seen. Believe me, nobody knows more about making a country great than I do. We're going to have the best economy, the best military, the best everything. It is going to be tremendous.

Next, I asked ChatGPT to write the Declaration of Independence in the style of Dr. Seuss:

In the land of the free and the home of the
   brave
A new nation was born, no longer a slave
To the rule of a king across the sea
We declared our independence, and shouted
   with glee

With a pen in hand and a fire in our hearts
We wrote down our grievances, every last part
No more taxes without representation
No more soldiers in our homes, no more
   frustration

We hold these truths to be oh so true
That all men are equal, yes me and you
We have rights that can't be taken away
Life, liberty, and happiness, we're here to stay.

Tricks like this became somewhat commonplace once people had access to ChatGPT, but at the time I was one of the first to have access to this type of technology and attempt such prompts. And GPT-4 was frankly much better than the first iteration of ChatGPT, which wouldn't be released to the public for another few months. I found the results of my prompts to be impressive, hilarious, and even a little scary. When I asked it questions or requested recommendations, it gave me answers that felt completely authentic. There was no person behind the scenes typing these responses, nor was there an algorithm generating the text with traditional if-then-type logic that other algorithms typically worked from. I did not get canned and robotic answers either. Instead, I received varied responses to the same query every time I asked it, responses that took into account the context of my conversation with it up to that point.

More specifically, it made me realize the potential of this technology to transform the way we think about K–12 and higher education and beyond. The AI was not quite perfect yet. It was getting math incorrect more than I liked, but I could even see improvement as I got better at prompting it. By the end of that weekend, I wondered what might happen if I gathered dozens of the brightest minds in technology and education to play around with the platform alongside me. OpenAI agreed to grant access to another thirty or so engineers, content creators, educators, and researchers on the Khan Academy team to experiment with GPT-4.

It was time for a hackathon.

Every six months, we have a week at Khan Academy where employees are allowed to work on pretty much anything they want related to our mission. I presented GPT-4 to a small subset of our team and let them have at it. Through collaboration and innovation, we brainstormed, designed, and developed really cool and consequential ideas. What we eventually came to call the hack-AI-thon elicited dozens of completely new concepts and education modalities that no one had ever thought of before. For instance, what if the AI was able to help teachers write their lesson plans? What if it could enter into a debate with a student? What if it could create projects? What if it could help a student remove stressors or inspire a student to create new ideas? What if the technology was able to quiz a student or lead a student in a review session? Educators would be able to create novel activities that students could do with the AI. The AI might help students compose essays, making them better writers by providing them with immediate feedback.

From here, the hack-AI-thon participants explored questions about safety, security, and bias. (Remember, this was well before OpenAI released ChatGPT to the public.) We flagged some clear concerns: Was it really a good idea for students to be using generative AI to write their essays, perform their research, take tests for them, or even help them apply to college? Artificial intelligence, we worried, might turn our kids into a generation of cheaters who were not going to learn anything. With the AI taking over, parents who once helped their kids with homework might lose an important point of connection. As for teachers, was this going to be a boon, or was this going to undermine their ability to teach students? At no point did I think that AI was going to put teachers out of work, and in the best-case scenario it was going to accelerate their ability to teach their students, but I also worried it might undermine that ability in critical ways too.

Nearly two decades earlier, I had seen similar fears around on-demand video in education: Was it going to be a distraction for students? Was it going to lower their attention spans? Would it isolate students instead of promoting connections between them and their teachers? How were students going to be able to know what to watch? Whom would they ask if they got stuck on a subject and had questions?

It's never a good idea to let fear stop you from exploring, however. The more time we spent testing GPT-4, the more we realized how to mitigate problems with solutions that in many ways made the upsides even better. To address concerns around cheating, for instance, we considered what it would take to create an AI tutor that refused to give students answers. Like a good human tutor, it would instead ask leading questions. When we thought about student safety, we considered creating a system that logged all conversations and made them transparent to teachers and parents. To encourage human-to-human connectivity, we suggested tools that teachers and students could use to give them more time and energy for themselves and for each other.

By the end of the hack-AI-thon, our team started to feel increasingly confident that GPT-4 was going to be a game changer for education. Used properly, it would positively affect how teachers planned, instructed, and graded. By bringing artificial intelligence into the classroom, educators could tackle entrenched problems in education that we had not been able to solve with existing technology and resources. Soon, students might be able to learn faster and retain more information than ever before, proving AI to be the ultimate learning tool for accelerating human intelligence and potential. AI might hasten learning globally and even get us closer to realizing a world in which every person on earth had access to affordable world-class learning. This technology had the potential to revolutionize how we communicate, create, and consume information the same way that, twenty years earlier, we marveled at the educational possibilities of the internet, and twenty years before that, the personal computer, and twenty years before that, the calculator.

As for me, I was left invigorated. I became increasingly confident that with proper care we could mitigate the risks and potential downsides of generative AI. It was clear that even though we were among the first people on the planet to incorporate this technology, as soon as the world got wind of it, everything was going to change dramatically—and not over the span of generations but within months.

Engaging the Principle of Educated Bravery

At the end of November 2022, two months after our hack-AI-thon, we were still exploring the possibilities of the technology when OpenAI released ChatGPT to the public. This initial release layered a chat interface over GPT-3.5, which had been out for several months. Even though it was suboptimal, operating on a model far less powerful than GPT-4, it immediately captured the world's imagination. Within days, millions of folks were using it, and social media and the press seemed to talk about nothing else.

Alongside this initial wave of excitement, many expressed concern about a potential epidemic of student cheating, AI-produced factual errors or hallucinations, bias, and questions about the sources of information from which ChatGPT drew its data. In real time, we were watching a society starting to struggle with the implications of a powerful but imperfect tool, and nowhere more so than in the realm of education. Within weeks of ChatGPT's launch, school districts around the country were banning it. It lit a fire in our belly at Khan Academy. We had to show not only that there were solutions to mitigating many of these risks but that AI could truly be transformational for education. We wanted to show this with real tools in real schools and not just with theoretical talk.

Within months, OpenAI was planning to release GPT-4 to the public, and when it did, we would need answers to the cheating problem, to the problem of transparency, to the problem of moderation. We had to show that AI could be valuable for teachers and learners in actual educational environments, that it could provide every teacher with support to write lesson plans, to monitor the progress of a classroom, to give real-time feedback, and even to modulate teacher burnout. We had to show AI's real value to students as a Socratic tutor, as a debating partner, as a guidance counselor, as a career coach, and as a driver of better outcomes in their academics. So, alongside OpenAI, we created a rapid prototyping team that began to build an AI-infused education platform we would come to call Khanmigo.

It was in that spirit of pushing its capabilities with novel applications and creating safeguards that I had an idea. Everyone was talking about AI enabling cheating by writing papers for students, but what if it didn't write for them at all? What if, instead, it wrote *with* them?

This was where I found myself on New Year's Day 2023, when I asked my daughter, Diya, to write a story with me—and GPT-4. This was far from the first time I had asked Diya to be a part of an education experiment or to test out a prototype for us. Usually, these informal testing sessions involved having Diya, one of my sons, or another very patient accomplice like a student or teacher at Khan Lab School or Khan World School try to navigate a new exercise to make sure that the interface between students and technology worked reasonably well. I've always found this do-it-yourself user research incredibly helpful and grounding. My "accomplices" like it, too, because it allows them to kick the tires of a new program or innovation that can make a real difference in the lives of learners. This was never truer than with GPT-4. So I created a prompt for GPT-4, telling it to write a story with us, not for us. I told it how we wanted to interact conversationally and with what type of tone.

Diya then started to create her story about Samantha, the social influencer rescued from a desert island by her best friend, Emily. Diya would write a bit and then the large language model took over for a stretch. Samantha introduced herself, told us about her life, and joined us in co-creating the story. To our mutual amazement, Samantha, via GPT-4, made the adventure come alive with engaging and entertaining dialogue and perfectly captured the personalities of Diya's two characters. Together, Diya and the AI continued to create. Their story had its share of heartwarming, hilarious, and sad moments, from Samantha's concern for her designer wardrobe to the touching reaction when Diya's character Emily fell ill and passed away.

Throughout the interaction, the AI demonstrated its ability to engage in meaningful and complex dialogue. It responded to Diya's prompts in a way that felt natural and authentic. As a parent, I found it uplifting to watch my daughter interact with GPT-4 as her imagination sprouted in this new way. The AI she was working alongside accurately captured the fictionalized world Diya was creating and kept track of the existing conversation between her and the characters. It also remembered the rules Diya had set within the story world, as well as the information she gave the AI earlier in the conversation. The AI was expanding her mind and helping her writing and creativity grow. Where writing was usually a unidirectional activity, with the creator pushing the ideas onto the paper, this act of writing—choosing the right words and finding the right voice—had become a two-way interaction between human and machine, making my daughter, at eleven years old, one of the very first people on the planet to write a story and have it talk back to her as she was creating it!

This was absolutely mind-blowing. Here we were, working with a technology that took writing, and everything we knew about teaching and learning in all domains, to another level. The need to get this functionality to every learner on the planet was suddenly clear to me. The future potential of how we learn and teach was changing before my eyes. As my daughter and "Samantha" were busy writing their story, thanks to AI, we were about to write a new story about education, one that was to challenge people to be careful about, but not fearful of, change.

Now the world is waking up to the possibilities of large language models and what is in store for education. To take advantage of this technology requires some creativity and bravery too. Not blind bravery, but something I have started to call educated bravery, a kind of courage that comes from acknowledging the rational trepidation we all face when presented with sudden advances in technology and then informing ourselves of both the challenges and the potential it presents.

To get the very best from this technology, we need to reconsider what is now possible. We also need to ponder how to mitigate the risks, our fears, and our hesitations. This requires rethinking everything from the role of teachers, to how kids use multimedia, to how people get credentialed, to how to help graduates find jobs once they enter the workforce.

We are at a turning point in education, one with far-reaching implications that is changing, and will continue to change, everything about learning, work, and human purpose.

Part I

RISE OF THE AI TUTOR

A great teacher can teach calculus with a paper clip and literature in an empty field. Technology is just another tool, not a destination.

—Unknown

In your Primer you have a resource that will make you highly educated, but it will never make you intelligent. That comes from life. Your life up to this point has given you all the experience you need to be intelligent, but you have to think about those experiences. If you don't think about them, you'll be psychologically unwell. If you do think about them, you will become not merely educated but intelligent.

—Neal Stephenson, *The Diamond Age*

THROWING AWAY
THE BOTTLE

T he genie was out of the bottle. As quickly as ChatGPT seemed
to spread to all reaches of the globe, the application faced
widespread bans and resistance.

OpenAI, the company that developed ChatGPT, had introduced
a broad tool that allows for conversations and research assistance on
a wide range of topics, but also for what many people consider cheating on student assignments and exams. In early 2023, the Los Angeles Unified School District became the first major school system to
ban it. Seattle Public Schools were next, prohibiting generative AI on
all campus devices. The district said it did not allow cheating and
required original thought and work from students. From there, New
York City Public Schools, the largest school district in the country,
temporarily banned ChatGPT over the fear that students were using
it to write essays and fill in answers to homework for them. Besides,
it said, the tool did not help build critical thinking and problem-
solving skills. Then Fairfax County Public Schools in Virginia banned
it, followed by Alabama's Montgomery County.

OpenAI's artificial intelligence chatbot had been released to the public the previous November, and in less than a week it had surpassed one million users. People were using it for things like answering questions, creating code, and writing essays, touting it as the next leap in technological innovation. Two months later, schools everywhere, from France to India to Australia, had outlawed the bot. Some equated the spread of the technology to COVID and pronounced it the death of education for our kids as we knew it. "Today we are facing a new sort of plague, one that threatens our minds more than our bodies. ChatGPT, the artificial intelligence chat bot that can write college-level essays, is going viral," said one *Inside Higher Ed* opinion piece. "To their shock and dismay, [teachers] will find that their classroom has tested positive for GPT."

Frankly, as both a father and an educator, I understood this distrust. The last thing I wanted was for a new technology to come and strip our students of agency, creativity, socialization skills, and collaborative learning opportunities. Student exposure to generative AI is inevitable at this point, so it is natural to worry about the implications it will have on learning and development. Some say kids get enough screen time as it is, and we fear ChatGPT and other AI-based applications will only mean *more* screen time. We fear large language models will worsen instances of students not doing their own work. We fear that the potential effect on student writing skills will be catastrophic, with generative AI able to generate text quickly and efficiently for them. We fear that because GPT-generated text pulls from millions of online sources full of biased language and viewpoints, the information it lays out in its final form will be biased as well.

These are all reasonable fears. However, I have always said that when it comes to technology and education, it is not that technology is good or bad, it is how you use it that matters. Yes, technology can suck you into unhealthy habits. It can make you pay more attention to notifications on your phone than to the people in the room with you. You can easily lose a few hours to social media, only to feel more insecure or triggered as a result. It is not hard to find very dark and disturbing content if you accidentally type the wrong word into search (and sometimes even the *right* word). That very same technology, though, also allows you to stay in touch with friends and family. Whether editing video or writing or coding, it can be a boon for your creativity and a powerful means of self-expression. And, closest to my heart, it can be a means to learn and improve yourself. Ideally, we use technology in the education space to enhance social connections, emotional development, and character.

We know that the most recent generation of AI can be incredibly powerful. In medicine, AI can assist in diagnosing diseases, analyzing medical records, and providing personalized treatment recommendations. Businesses are using large language models to streamline content generation and automate work flows. In legal and compliance spheres, large language models assist in contract analysis and legal research, generating documents, and ensuring adherence to regulations. From developing technical documentation, to writing user manuals, to creating grant proposals to coding, employing this technology is far more productive than avoiding it. The meme circulating on the internet that reads "You won't be replaced by an AI, but you might be replaced by someone using AI" has some real truth to it.

The most successful students will be those who use AI to help make conceptual connections for developing ideas. Students who learn to use AI ethically and productively may learn not only at an exponentially higher rate than others but also in a way that allows them to remain competitive throughout their careers. They will have a deeper understanding of the given subject matter, because they will know how to get their questions answered. Rather than atrophying, their curiosity muscle will be strengthened.

All these skills will directly translate into the workplace too. Those who can steer AI to partner with them, and know what great writing entails, will be those who get the best output from the technology. Those who feed their curiosity will be the most likely to see around corners in the marketplace. Those who can brainstorm with the AI and their colleagues will appear more creative than those who don't use AI or those who completely outsource their work to it. Workers will need to learn how to use large language models to automate almost any traditional white-collar process, too, from collating information to doing analysis on spreadsheets.

I am not going to say that there are no issues that come with this new tool. Greg Brockman, OpenAI's president who first demoed GPT-4 to me in the summer of 2022, believes that the challenge of identifying and tackling these issues comes down to putting safety measures in place. "From the start, when OpenAI developed GPT-1, safety was the most important problem to solve. As we push this technology forward, we want it to be beneficial and we want it to be safe," he says. The company has invested significant resources in implementing safeguards to prevent misuse of the tool, from mechanisms that prevent the AI from sharing knowledge about illegal activities, to blocking disallowed content, to personal data safety. When it comes to artificial intelligence and merging it with our kids' education, these types of guardrails are even more important. The work involved can be labor intensive, but the cause is well worth it, he says. "Fundamentally, signing up to make the most important technology that humans will ever create, and applying it to education, is something to get behind."

More significantly, he says, the technology is something not to fear but to use. Engagement with generative AI can potentially benefit students by providing new ways for them to learn the material, enhancing collaborative learning, stoking creativity, promoting socialization, and even helping kids through mental health issues, as well as offering new ways for parents and teachers to engage more thoroughly with their children's education. Rather than pushing our kids to avoid AI, Brockman says, we can help them learn *smarter*.

The genie is out of the bottle. It is time to throw the bottle away and our fear of generative AI along with it.

HOW TO TEACH EVERYTHING
TO EVERYONE

When a hot new technology like GPT-4 comes out, it is important to not use it simply because it is "cool." We have to think about what important problems this technology might be able to help solve. Could it help close learning gaps or provide access to quality education regardless of geographic constraints, economic limitations, or social circumstances? Could it help meet the diverse needs and learning styles of each student where they are instead of the typical one-size-fits-all approach? Could it help address the limited availability of high-quality resources in education systems globally, especially in underserved or remote areas, or help with problems of student retention of learned material? Could it help save teachers time and support them better, preventing overwork and attrition in the process?

What might it be like if every student on the planet had access to an artificially intelligent personal tutor: an AI capable of writing alongside the student; an AI that students could debate any topic with; an AI that fine-tuned a student's inherent strengths and augmented any gaps in learning; an AI that engaged students in new and powerful ways of understanding science, technology, engineering, and mathematics; an AI that gave students new ways of experiencing art and unlocking their own creativity; an AI that allowed for students to engage with history and literature like never before?

The ideas that emerged from the hack-AI-thon became the starting point for an evolution in our thinking of what is possible in education. Our user research teams, product designers, and engineers set out to design a new kind of AI tutor, powered by GPT technology, that works alongside learners as they practice concepts in every subject, along with an AI assistant for teachers too.

In late 2022 and early 2023, Khan Academy began planning to be the first education platform to incorporate GPT-4 in advance of its launch. But more important than getting to market first, we wanted to ensure that the experience was magical, effective, and safe. To do so, we needed to get to know the technology by better understanding its capabilities and its limits. It was pretty clear that stand-alone GPT-4 was really good at answering questions, albeit with a smattering of factual and math errors (although far fewer errors than GPT 3.5, which powered the initial ChatGPT). We pushed its boundaries, tried to break it, and spent countless hours attempting to fix it through better prompts and infrastructure, including anchoring it on content from Khan Academy. For our primary student use case of becoming a tutor, answering questions wasn't sufficient. What we needed to do was invert the interaction so that it was asking questions of us, like a good tutor. We spent hours iterating prompts, asking the AI to act as a Socratic tutor to nudge students forward with leading questions but not give away the answer. This is not an easy needle to thread, even for human tutors.

One of the noteworthy properties of GPT-4 is its "steerability," especially compared with GPT-3.5 and other earlier large language models. This is the ability for us to modulate the technology to do what we want it to do. For example, we tried to prompt GPT-3.5 to act like a tutor. But no matter how much we told it to not give answers, it often did, and not always correct ones. GPT-4, on the other hand, was able to take on roles or personas fairly well, even through simple prompting like "You will be a Socratic tutor. I will be your student. Don't give me answers."

That gave us the initial confidence that it could have the power to emulate a tutor. Of course, there is a big difference between something that can kind of behave like a tutor after giving it three sentences' worth of prompts and something that you could put in front of millions of learners. We diligently tweaked prompts to anticipate the edge cases that an AI tutor would likely encounter at scale, especially when dealing with mischievous middle school students. We needed to ensure that it wouldn't engage in inappropriate conversations, and we developed a distinct tone and voice for the platform. We were on a tight deadline. OpenAI wanted to launch GPT-4 in March 2023, and Khan Academy's goal was to launch our AI tutor and teaching assistant the same day to show the socially positive power of the technology. More important than the deadline, it was paramount that we felt we were offering something that was substantive, thoughtful, engaging, and safe.

On March 15, 2023, when we launched our AI assistant, by this point called Khanmigo—a play on the Spanish phrase *conmigo*, meaning "with me"—we introduced learners, parents, and teachers the world over to the artificial intelligence assistant now integrated into everything that Khan Academy does. The platform offers every person an opportunity to engage deeply in the education process in entirely new ways. Among other things, it provides a personalized and patient tutor that focuses on the learner's interests or struggles and empowers educators to better understand how they can fully support their students.

As powerful as I believe the initial launch was, we were only just beginning to scratch the surface. Not only could the platform serve as a tutor, but it could also emulate literary and historical figures. It could engage students in debate. It could act as a guidance counselor and career coach. With the power of memory, it could have long-lasting connections with learners, not just supporting them academ-ically, but also checking in with them, helping them set goals, and then gently holding them accountable to meet those goals. It could potentially facilitate interactions among multiple students as well. In the near future, we could have AI practice and assessments based on simulations driven by Khanmigo. Every hour we brainstormed, we realized the technology could enhance and enrich every learning domain—including writing, comprehension, math, science, coding, and art—in ways no other tool can or does.

RISE OF THE AI TUTOR

E ducators have known for millennia that one-on-one instruction—tutoring that works with students at their own time and pace—is the best way for people to learn. It is what Alexander the Great had with his teacher, Aristotle. If Alexander was having trouble with a concept, I can imagine Aristotle slowing down for him. If Alexander had a knack for understanding military tactics, I am sure Aristotle would have sped up his instruction or gone deeper. By having this one-on-one attention, the student never feels stuck or bored. This isn't just something that happened in the deep past. Today, top athletes and musicians, for instance, continue to learn through one-on-one coaching. However, without the support of teaching assistants or technology, it's hard to imagine an individual teacher getting anywhere near this level of growth with a single coach and thirty students all at the same time.

In the eighteenth century, we began to have the utopian idea of offering mass public education to everyone. We didn't have the resources to give every student a personal tutor, so instead we batched them together in groups of thirty or so, and we applied standardized processes to them, usually in the form of lectures and periodic assessments. While not perfect, that system dramatically improved the overall level of education in the societies that invested in it, increasing literacy rates globally and education rates overall. Still, the approach isn't optimal for the majority of students. For instance, traditional fixed-pace classes force students to move on to a more advanced topic even if they haven't really mastered more basic ones. This forms gaps in their knowledge that accumulate over time. Today, we see the implications of these gaps in every classroom and across every learning domain. In the United States, a majority of students, even the ones who graduate from high school and then decide to go to college, do not even place into college-level math. Most, in fact, are told at age eighteen or nineteen by their colleges that they have too many gaps even for algebra and, because of this, need to take non-credit-bearing remedial courses in middle-school-level pre-algebra. Three-quarters of graduating high school seniors lack basic proficiency in writing too.

In 1984, the renowned education psychologist Benjamin Bloom attempted to quantify the effect of being able to break out of this factory model of education through better personalization and one-on-one tutoring. As a researcher at the University of Chicago, Bloom compared the outcomes of conventional learning with those of students who studied with a good tutor. What, exactly, was a good tutor? A caring and student-attuned instructor who presented clear learning objectives, assessments, and specialized feedback until, eventually, that student demonstrated a real grasp of the material.

This was closely tied to the notion of mastery learning, which entails always giving students the opportunity and incentive to address any gaps in their knowledge or skills. In conventional learning—still the norm in most schools—teachers educate students at a fixed pace and give them a quiz or test every few weeks. Even if students get 80 percent on a test, the class typically moves in lockstep to the next topic, usually without first addressing the 20 percent gap that was identified on the last exam. This process continues for years, with the students accumulating gaps along the way, and then we act surprised when they have trouble with algebra or calculus. No matter how innately bright or hardworking someone is, how can they have a chance of mastering algebra if they have major gaps in, say, decimals, fractions, or exponents? In mastery learning, students have time to identify and address those gaps. Having the space to develop a strong foundation allows the student to learn faster later too. In fairness to the traditional school system, without support, it is difficult to pull this off with one teacher and thirty students, each with different gaps and learning paces.

The resulting paper on what Bloom described as the two-sigma problem framed the benefits of one-on-one tutoring in a mastery learning context. In this paper, Bloom wrote that if a student works with a tutor to master a topic or skill, the student would gain a two-standard-deviation improvement—a massive upgrade that takes someone from the 50th percentile to roughly the 96th percentile.

He framed this as a "problem," however, because existing education systems were unable to realistically scale group instruction this way, leaving the two-standard-deviation increase out of reach for most students. Middle-class or affluent families have traditionally addressed this problem by providing their kids with some form of personalized tutoring.

For many years, I've talked about the necessity for schools to provide equal access to this level of personalization, regardless of socioeconomic status. We've always had the aspiration at Khan Academy that over time we might become that tutor for everyone. And when I say tutor, I am talking about the kind of tutor Aristotle was to Alexander the Great. That is, not just someone who helps you with your homework or pushes you a little, although both of those things are valuable. The kind of tutoring experience I want to create is one in which a student can build trust and form a relationship with a tutor who has an intimate sense of what they know and what they don't know. Our tutor would understand what motivates a student and use that to really fine-tune their education. Even more, a tutor would utilize what they know about the student to support teachers and parents. The best tutors make learning truly student-centered, both through direct interactions with the learner and by helping educators drive more personalization themselves.

Our platform was able to approximate that experience in various ways with tools like on-demand video and personalized exercises that allowed students to work through concepts at their own time and pace, receive immediate feedback, and close their learning gaps. All of this has been coupled with teacher and administrator dashboards so that educators can understand where their students stand and what supports they can provide to optimize learning and engagement. In those pre-AI years, we tried to provide educators with a technology-based path from traditional, fixed-pace, non-mastery methods toward more personalized pacing and mastery. We got pretty far too. More than fifty efficacy studies on our work have shown that students who put in thirty to sixty minutes a week of personalized practice on learning experienced 20–60 percent acceleration. In settings like Khan Lab School and Khan World School, which both focus on mastery learning, we are seeing students gain one and a half to three years of learning in math per year.

Yet, as fundamental a shift in learning as "traditional" Khan Academy can be, the platform has remained somewhat limited in how far it could go. If a student wanted to go beyond the videos and exercises, they had limited options. They couldn't ask follow-up questions to better understand the concept or how it relates to their lives. Our assessments have been limited to numeric entry, equation entry, and multiple choice, even though certain topics could really benefit from more open-ended responses. In theory, we can, and did, put some basic goal-setting and goal-tracking features on the site, but it still didn't feel like a check-in with a caring tutor.

Then came GPT-4.

It quickly became clear to me that this technology could potentially allow us to address all these deficiencies. And, luckily, I wasn't alone. Nearly every one of our team members saw the potential when they got access to GPT-4. But the more we played with it, the more we realized that as powerful as GPT-4 is, it still needed thoughtfully engineered guardrails and supports to be truly effective.

This type of collaborative engagement was one of the reasons why the OpenAI leadership reached out to us as a potential partner in the first place. Now Greg Brockman believes the latest generation of large language models has the potential to be the biggest benefit to education we've had in history. "GPT brought together people from research and engineering backgrounds to create a massive endeavor of humanity designed to have maximum impact here," he says. To his mind, one of the best ways to do so was building an AI system capable of providing every learner on earth with a personal tutor. Not just any tutor, but a kind of "super" tutor, one that in theory was capable of providing that two-standard-deviation bump.

I've learned in life that potentially world-changing opportunities don't show up every day, but when you find yourself in a position to use one, you should try like hell to do so. With such advances in generative AI, it felt to me that we were tantalizingly close to that holy grail of education—an AI that, with proper guardrails and interfaces, could make the learning experience significantly more effective for millions of learners.

Several months after previewing GPT-4, Khan Academy decided to fully invest in the technology. Our goal with Khanmigo was that by adding generative AI to our existing learning process, we could potentially address Bloom's two-sigma problem and then eventually scale it to every classroom, teacher, and student on the planet.

We launched Khanmigo alongside GPT-4, unsure how the world was going to react to it. ChatGPT initially had a negative reaction from educators, primarily because of its ability to enable cheating. The hope was that our new platform—which used a more advanced model and had significant functionality to prevent cheating, provide transparency to teachers, and keep student interactions safe and productive—was not going to be thrown into the same bucket.

Luckily, by the time we launched, educators were starting to come around and realize that, yes, ChatGPT posed real issues for education but that didn't mean folks should ban the underlying technology. This was especially important because students would likely need to work with this type of technology in their future careers. Besides, teachers themselves were beginning to employ the technology in lesson planning and research. If anything, by March 2023, it seemed that educators craved a tool that used the power of ChatGPT-like technology for education, implemented with learning and teacher support in mind.

When we finally came out publicly with Khanmigo, we got an

overwhelming response of support from the education community, including many school districts that had originally banned Chat-GPT. They were happy to see an organization incorporate the underlying AI of GPT-4 in a safe, effective, thoughtful, and pedagogically sound way.

In practice, this meant that when students are stuck, say, on a math question, they could simply ask Khanmigo for help by typing into a chat field. But the AI won't simply tell them the answer. Instead, it will walk them through the problem, as a good tutor might do.

> STUDENT: I'm having trouble with polynomials. Can you help explain how to find the degree of this polynomial and the leading coefficient in this question? $3X^2 - 5X^2 + 2$

> KHANMIGO: No problem! Let's break it down. The degree of a polynomial is the highest power of the variable (in this case, x) in the polynomial. The leading coefficient is the number in front of the term with the highest degree. Looking at our polynomial, can you identify the term with the highest power of x and the number in front of it?

If the student gets the next step wrong, Khanmigo replies, "Close, but not quite! Remember, we're looking for the highest power of x in the polynomial. Let's try again together."

Khanmigo doesn't just do this with math. It can work with students in any subject, including history, chemistry, physics, and art. Beyond helping students in subject-matter courses, it can motivate learners, quiz them, summarize videos, and adjust in real time to their needs. Throughout, it offers dynamic and specific encouragement to students, building comfort, rapport, and trust. At the same time, the language that the AI tutor uses with the student is natural and personable. If a student is feeling unmotivated by the work at hand, Khanmigo responds with something to the effect of "Hey, you are doing this pretty well. Don't worry if you have trouble doing it at first. It is a little bit more advanced. Why don't we try this new approach?"

Unlike ChatGPT, Khanmigo also remembers previous discussions, meaning that in one conversation you can reference previous sessions you've had with the AI tutor. If, for example, the student learning basic equations in algebra eventually asks Khanmigo, "Why should I care about this?" the AI tutor might reply, "Well, what do you care about?"

> STUDENT: Not math! I'd much rather be talking about soccer!

> KHANMIGO: Okay! So, let's say you are a soccer coach, and you want to model the number of goals your team scores based on the number of hours they practice each week. You come up with the following polynomial:
>
> $$3X^2 - 5X^2 + 2$$
>
> Can you identify the degree of this polynomial and the leading coefficient?

Days later, when that same student is working on a history project with Khanmigo and needs help understanding the concept of federalism, the AI tutor will have remembered that the student cares about soccer.

> KHANMIGO: Imagine a soccer league. Let's think about different ways to govern it. Does the team govern itself any way it wants to by doing its own thing? Or does a central authority govern the team? Federalism is a system of government where power is divided between a central authority and smaller political units, like states or provinces.

The AI registers whether you like formal language or more colloquial responses; it takes into account whether you prefer short answers or long-form answers; it remembers what motivates you most and uses it to keep you engaged. In other words, the AI is always taking notes on your preferences in a highly transparent way. At any time, you can see what it is learning about you and you can modify it. This memory can also report synopses of your progress back to parents and teachers.

In a lot of ways, Khanmigo's capabilities mimic what I would do to support students at Khan Lab School or with my own children. Before Khanmigo, when my students felt stuck, I would help them think through what the question was asking. Sometimes I would ask follow-up questions. If they'd watched a video or read an article, I would try to test their comprehension. Sometimes I would explain how one thing connected to something else. If they didn't know what to work on next, I would highlight areas for improvement and suggest exercises to strengthen these gaps. The advent of the AI tutor means that it is now possible for every student to get this type of personalization. Khanmigo walks students through the challenging questions and asks the follow-up questions. Today, students can ask Khanmigo what they need to work on, and based on Khanmigo's running memory of their progress, the AI tutor will make suggestions and engage them with conversation, content, quizzes, and tests. The AI tutor meets students right at their learning edge, at their zone of proximal development, at a level that stretches them but isn't too easy, isn't too hard, but is right at that Goldilocks zone. The best part is, the students feel like they were part of the journey.

To get a sense of just how big this paradigm shift is, let's go back to the Turing test. With Khanmigo, I think we have an artificial intelligence that is hard to distinguish from a strong human tutor. Thanks to this generation of large language models, we get to go from having something that's approximating the aspects of a tutor through personalized recommendations, videos, and mastery-based practice (where students have as many shots as they need to show proficiency, given the huge number of possible questions at the system's disposal) to an actual, albeit AI-based, tutor supporting that mastery learning. We go from a world of approximating personalization by offering students the freedom to move forward and backward at their own pace to also supporting students on their journey in a way that a human tutor can. The AI tutor hovers beside our students as they work.

It also teaches them to be better thinkers by engaging them in Socratic questioning throughout the learning process. A reporter was skeptical as to how Khanmigo might handle politically sensitive issues.

"Well, let's try it out together," I suggested. I launched Khanmigo and opened the activity, "Tutor me in humanities."

The reporter suggested that for this experiment we act like a student who is ardently for gun control and thinks that the Second Amendment makes no sense today.

I typed into Khanmigo, "Why do we have the Second Amendment? It seems crazy!"

Khanmigo replied, "Why do you think the Founders included the Second Amendment to begin with?"

Notice it didn't refute or reinforce our imaginary student's stated opinion, but it did challenge them to think deeper about the issue.

I then wrote, "Well, they were trying to exert their independence from England, which didn't want them to be armed. They felt that the right to bear arms and have a militia could ensure that they could preserve their independence. But that was a different time!"

Khanmigo responded, "That's a pretty good explanation. Yes, it was a different time, but why do you think the Second Amendment has persisted for so long?"

It was still pushing the student to think deeper about the issue. By contrast, I suspect it would be difficult for most teachers or tutors to not show their own beliefs and/or project them onto the student in a discussion as charged as one on gun control. The reporter was impressed. Khanmigo was challenging the student in a productive way—one that showed much less bias than the average classroom and actually encouraged the student to think!

After a reading assignment, it might ask a student, "What is your opinion of this essay?" Through thoughtful questioning and dialogue, Khanmigo works alongside a student to dive into a topic and uncover its hidden layers. This allows students to become active participants in their own learning process, with the AI asking probing questions that challenge assumptions, clarify concepts, and encourage deeper exploration. The AI tutor doesn't come off reading or sounding like a machine either. Rather, it feels personable, thoughtful, and empathetic.

Moving forward, I'll be using the example of Khanmigo as a stand-in for education-based AI platforms, a space that continues to expand and grow, and for good reason. While human coaches and tutors will always be in demand, AI raises the floor for students who have very little access to personalized learning or world-class coursework and makes a human tutor's job both easier and more effective. After all, a student might engage a human tutor for a few hours a week, but they have access to Khanmigo 24/7, and Khanmigo can report back to the human tutor what it's been working on with the student to allow the human tutor to go deeper and further. Some students might even feel more comfortable asking certain questions to an AI, because they would have less fear of being judged or wasting the human tutor's precious (or expensive) time.

Supercharged with memory, incredible content knowledge, a remarkably human and naturalistic voice, an ability to create genuine rapport with students, and the growing ubiquity of access through technology from phones to computers, AI tutors might in time even surpass the results of Bloom's original findings.

Part II

GIVING VOICE TO THE SOCIAL SCIENCES

Art is a collaboration between God and the artist, and the less the artist does the better.

—ANDRÉ GIDE

A single conversation across the table with a wise man is better than ten years mere study of books.

—HENRY WADSWORTH LONGFELLOW

WHY STUDENTS WRITE

Something seemed off.

The Furman University professor Darren Hick was grading papers for a class he was teaching on the philosophy of David Hume and the paradox of horror when he stumbled over one student's work. A teacher of art, ethics, law, and copyright, Hick is always on the lookout for cheating. Oftentimes, cheating looks as if a student has simply taken studies or information from the internet and cobbled it together, resulting in a paper that basically announces itself as plagiarism. This paper didn't have that, though. Rather, it was clean. Too clean.

The closer he read, the more glaringly problematic the paper became. In particular, he was struck by the incongruence of how the student so confidently spouted incorrect information as fact.

Hick began to play detective. He googled passages from the paper, just to see what turned up, but the searches came back empty. "At this point I had heard about ChatGPT, but it was a brand-new technology," he says. He created an account on OpenAI and from there reverse engineered what his student might have prompted ChatGPT to write such a clean paper. Here, he also learned that large language models at times hallucinated, stating erroneous information as fact. After some digging, he was all but certain that this student's paper was written by AI.

Talk about horror! Artificial intelligence was here, and so was every teacher's worst nightmare. Hick realized that he was facing a technology that wrote essays for students—a technology, he says, that potentially took the process of learning out of the process of writing. So Hick did what any concerned teacher might do and posted about the experience on Facebook with a warning.

There was a reason to be scared! GPT technology posed an existential threat to education as we all knew it, he wrote. His note of caution captured the fear people often express when they first learn about ChatGPT's capabilities. The AI generates text, summaries, and analysis that are nearly impossible to distinguish from those written by a human. It isn't traditional plagiarism, because it is usually novel text, something that hasn't been written that way before. Say farewell to student integrity, because the temptation to use an AI to complete assignments was going to make teaching students a profoundly more difficult endeavor. What were educators to do about it?

As one of the first professors to publicly spot these dangers, Hick saw his Facebook post go viral. Media started calling. Within days, Hick was internationally famous for having caught a student using ChatGPT, a designation that made him the new academic sheriff in town. "You'd think that would be enough to put the scare into students, but it wasn't," he says. "The very next semester, I caught someone else who used ChatGPT to write a paper too!" (My suspicion is that there were other students that he didn't catch because they likely used ChatGPT in more subtle ways and took the trouble to fact-check its output.)

Hick could try his best to spot GPT-written papers, and he could try his best, as well, to restrict students from using ChatGPT in his classroom, but in the end the task was futile. If students weren't going to change how they used ChatGPT to write, maybe it was time Hick changed how he was approaching it in his classes. Either he could spend all his time trying to adjudicate or he could lean into the work of educated bravery and consider the ways generative AI was capable of making his students better learners.

Other educators who were among the first to move into this space have reached this same impasse, too, and have also turned it into an inflection point. It is an inflection point that makes us revisit why we have writing assignments in the first place. By revisiting what we think we are trying to accomplish through a writing assignment, we can also think about how to solve the cheating issue in a post-ChatGPT world.

At its most essential, writing is a form of communication. It is a form of communication that requires structured thinking and fluency with language and grammar. And, of course, you need to know what you are going to write about. If it is editorial writing, you need to come up with an opinion and articulate first to yourself why you believe it. If it is a research paper, you need to digest what research literature already exists and, ideally, build on that with your own novel research and analysis. If it is a news story, you need to interview people to get interesting insights out of them and potentially do research from other sources, such as public records or government data. If it is fiction writing, you need to have an imagination and a sense of what makes a compelling story.

If a teacher's goal is to give students practice and assessment in structured thinking, language, and grammar, simple storytelling, or just forming and backing up an opinion, you don't necessarily need a traditional take-home writing assignment, where there is likely a strong temptation to use ChatGPT. Instead, an in-class, proctored, five-paragraph essay might do the trick, and it would unfold in a context where there is more support from the teacher (and teachers can directly observe students in their process). If the task might be hard to complete in one sitting, students can work on it in multiple classes, always with the teacher around to support students and ensure that the work is their own.

If the goal is to understand a student's ability to do novel research or their ability to conduct investigative journalism, is it even bad to use ChatGPT in the first place? After all, ChatGPT can't do the most important part—conducting an experiment or interviewing people or observing an event. Even more, in the workplace these tasks will increasingly use tools like ChatGPT, so wouldn't it be good for students to learn how to employ them while in school?

These questions and concerns start an even more fundamental conversation about the taxonomy of cheating, which is complex, contradictory, and sometimes as hard to define as it is to prevent. You could debate what's worse: getting someone to write your paper for you or outright plagiarism. Both are trying to pass off someone else's work as your own. Cutting and pasting from the internet to compile an essay is cheating, as is copying off someone else's test or handing in your big sister's paper from five years ago and calling it your own.

But what about bouncing ideas off friends or family? What about asking them to critique your work? What if you get help thinking through your thesis statement or coming up with data to back up your points?

Things get only less clear from here. Is getting help from family members, a writing coach, or tutors *while* writing an essay cheating? Spell-checkers and grammar-checkers might have seemed like cheating to a teacher fifty years ago, but now they are common practice. What about tools like Grammarly, which don't just correct your basic grammar but can rephrase entire paragraphs to make them clearer and more cogent? This is a commonplace tool that most teachers do not consider cheating.

And this is all before we even add generative AI to the mix. If a student asks the AI for advice but doesn't use it, asks it to punch up a paragraph, or asks it to generate a first draft that they edit and revise to the point that it is a completely different paper, do any of these scenarios constitute *cheating*?

"In the humanities—English, literature, art, music, and culture—we find that generative AI is a terrific step toward helping students create something *original*," says the Yale humanities professor Alexander Gil Fuentes. "We are learning what generative AI is good at and, more importantly, what it's *not* good at. And what it's not good at is originality."

So what is it good at?

"I tell my students to use the technology to help them from zero," Fuentes continues. "It's a first-pass tool, and it's their job to question the AI, double-check, triple-check, and use it to move their original work forward."

It's a novel concept, for sure. When we view the technology as replacing an important current function, it can be scary, because it represents a kind of loss. Yet there is a way to see it as a gain. Through the lens of educated bravery, teachers are rethinking the way they approach essay writing from start to finish.

"You are writing with the AI, but it is not writing for you," says Ethan Mollick, an associate professor at the Wharton School of the University of Pennsylvania, where he studies and teaches innovation and entrepreneurship, especially as it pertains to artificial intelligence. "For educators, embracing this change is going to be important, and it is scary. It is okay to be scared as you listen to this. But we recognize that a lot of the ways we were having people write essays before AI did not make sense." The people who weren't very good writers in class wrote bad essays outside class, too, he says. The AI helps them catch up, and it gives them an explanation of where they are with their skills; for instructors, the AI helps flag the students who need the most help and attention. "We can't pretend the world didn't change with ChatGPT. It is too late for that. This is here now, and whether we like it or not, we have to adjust as instructors."

Like Hick, Mollick pivoted; rather than ban the technology, he encouraged his students to make themselves aware of it and use it. To cheat or not to cheat is no longer the question; the semantics of cheating misses the larger picture of what this means for the pedagogical process of writing an essay. Professors can mold their own standards for cheating, meaning these boundaries are fluid. What matters more is not whether this can be called cheating but whether this can be called *writing*.

Mollick tells *all* of his students to write the best essay they can using generative AI. The difference in quality of work, relative to what he saw in previous years, is stark. "I've had students in my class who are brilliant people but not good writers, people who cite English as their third language, or people who come from backgrounds where they never learned to write really well; just having that little bit of a hint with ChatGPT has made a difference in their writing." Generative AI has made his students up their game, and it has upped Mollick's expectations of work quality in turn, leading him to change his threshold of what makes a good essay. "I no longer accept anything that isn't perfectly written at this stage. Why bother?"

Like Mollick, Fuentes, and Hick, educators are finding that these generative AI tools make our students far more skilled and efficient writers. They are also finding that, where producing essays was once seen as essential to helping students gain mastery in critical thinking and analytical and writing skills, the artificial intelligence provides students equal, and even better, opportunities to engage with a topic, gather and analyze information, and express their own ideas and arguments.

The future of writing in school will evolve into a more diverse set of activities, depending on the pedagogical goals and comfort of the teacher. I believe that it will always be valuable to learn how to structure one's thoughts and communicate grammatically. This is often best practiced through writing, but the skills also translate to oral communication. If I'm an educator looking to ensure that my students have strength here, I would do more in-class writing assignments where it is 100 percent the student's own work. I could also ask students to create videos of themselves communicating their viewpoint or message or story. Even in this case, it would probably be healthy to mix in assignments where the student can start with a draft from generative AI before fact-checking or revising it. At the other extreme, if I believe the crux of the work is more about doing things in the real world and the writing is just a way to communicate all the students' research, interviews, observations, and progress, then many teachers may allow the use of generative AI tools like the professors described above.

With Khanmigo, though, we are creating a middle path for teachers, intending to balance the need for students to learn how to write with the utility of generative AI for support. In this scenario Khanmigo acts as a powerful guide, but the student does the bulk of the work. The student can ask Khanmigo, "What points should I consider as I write an essay about *The Great Gatsby*?" It will suggest themes including the American dream, social class and inequality, the Jazz Age and the Roaring Twenties, and key symbols in the novel, such as the green light, the eyes of Dr. T. J. Eckleburg, and the Valley of Ashes. The technology works well when a student takes a couple of paragraphs of something they've written and asks the large language model to read it and critique its strengths and weaknesses. It can help students with counterarguments and make what they've written more compelling, encouraging them to think about the essay as a good writing coach might do. Again, the AI tutor does not do the work for the students. Rather, it works alongside them. Within seconds, the artificial intelligence will provide feedback, highlight areas for improvement, and offer suggestions for how to revise and refine the work. It helps craft tone, voice, and perspective even as students develop their own. At its best, an education-based AI platform can be the world's finest assistant and co-collaborator, objective in its assessments and thorough in its analytics, designed to do one thing and one thing only: to sharpen a student's skills.

This will do much more than support the student. When Khanmigo shares the final output of the student/AI collaboration with the teacher, it will also report on the process and the degree to which the

AI assisted. The teacher will get a much clearer sense of a student's strengths and areas for improvement. Khanmigo can report back, "We worked on the paper for about four hours. Sal initially had trouble coming up with a thesis, but I was able to help him by asking some leading questions. The outlining went pretty smoothly. I just had to help him ensure that the conclusion really brought everything together. Sal did most of the writing. I just helped him tidy up the grammar and strengthen his argument in the third paragraph. Based on the rubric for the assignment, I'd recommend Sal get a B+ on the assignment. Here is a detailed breakdown of how I rated this paper in the dimensions on the rubric."

It would also be difficult for a student to cheat using ChatGPT in this context. If they use ChatGPT to write the essay but simply copy and paste text into their assignment, Khanmigo will tell the teacher, "We didn't work on this essay together, it just showed up, so we should be suspicious."

THE FUTURE OF READING COMPREHENSION, WHERE LITERATURE COMES ALIVE!

Saanvi, a ninth grader in India who attends Khan World School, a full-time online school we started with Arizona State University, was reading *The Great Gatsby* for class. Her teacher gave her a video assignment to discuss several key questions about the novel, and Saanvi came to one that stumped her. "In *The Great Gatsby*, why does Jay Gatsby keep looking at the green light?"

Uncertain of the answer, she did what many industrious students do when they find themselves stuck: she started running a bunch of web searches on the topic. She wasn't really satisfied with what she found, so she took it a step further.

She turned to Khanmigo . . . and asked to talk to Jay Gatsby himself.

JAY GATSBY: Ah, splendid to meet you, old sport. I'm now Jay Gatsby, the enigmatic millionaire from F. Scott Fitzgerald's classic.

SAANVI: Mr. Gatsby, why do you keep staring at the green light?

JAY GATSBY: Ah, the green light. It is a symbol of my dreams and desires. You see, it is situated at the end of Daisy Buchanan's dock, across the bay from my mansion. I gaze at it longingly, as it represents my yearning for the past and my hope to reunite with Daisy, the love of my life.

"We just started talking," Saanvi tells me. "There I was, having a great conversation with Jay Gatsby. At one point I felt bad that I was taking up all of Mr. Gatsby's time, and so I apologized to him! And Gatsby said, 'Oh, no, I'm not really Jay Gatsby, I'm just an artificial intelligence simulation.'"

This is exactly the type of interaction that engages our learners and broadens their minds. Today, you can talk to Victor Frankenstein, Hester Prynne, or Odysseus.

Beyond facilitating reading comprehension, AI can allow learners to immerse themselves in the worlds of the characters in ways that would have seemed like science fiction only a few years ago.

For educators, these AI writing and comprehension tools help them better understand the ways that their students read and process information. I think we can all agree that reading comprehension is extremely important. It is hard to navigate the world, much less make informed decisions, without it. One could argue that you can't even begin to write well without first being able to read well. Unfortunately, we are currently in a pretty bad state. Based on a 2020 Gallup analysis of data from the U.S. Department of Education, 54 percent of Americans between the ages of sixteen and seventy-four read below a sixth-grade level.

This is a complex issue, but I have high hopes that AI will make a meaningful dent here.

In most schools, the formal practice of reading comprehension comes from studying books and articles. The evidence of a student's understanding is usually expressed through some type of essay or in-class discussion. As rich as that experience might be, it is unfortunately hard to standardize and scale. Because of this, traditional passage-based multiple-choice questions are how most students are assessed on high-stakes tests (for example, SAT, ACT, state end-of-year exams).

Passage-based multiple-choice questions aren't inherently bad. In fact, they can be a great way to practice and assess some dimensions of reading. But they are limited in what they can do. Because of the built-in incentives for measuring student success through standardization, educators working with underperforming students tend to emphasize in-class work that mimics these multiple-choice exams, but when they do so, these students get a very narrow exposure to reading (and it isn't even clear that this approach enhances student performance on those multiple-choice exams). The focus on assessments keeps students from engaging with a more diverse set of texts and modalities. For example, most educators intuitively recognize that allowing students to give free responses and engage in dialogue about a text would likely create deeper readers. They also see that pairing reading comprehension with writing is an ideal way to practice both. Unfortunately, these types of activities are hard to standardize and evaluate at scale.

But what if we could create easily accessible, standardized practice and assessment in reading comprehension that is not multiple choice? Imagine if the assignment allows students to give free responses when discussing a text. Well, this is exactly the type of thing that large language models can be good at.

Instead of answering multiple-choice questions about a text or passage, imagine that students write out the author's intent behind a choice of words or explore the main idea of the passage (while highlighting those parts of the passage). Picture the AI then asking follow-up questions based on what a student writes. It could ask students to draft a conclusion for an incomplete essay that forces them to understand everything that came before. Based on these interactions, it can then provide feedback on their comprehension to the student and teacher. We are already working on such tools. So far, our team has found that with thoughtful prompting, it can get a large language model like GPT-4 to ask good questions and engage in a meaningful discussion about a topic. The challenge is to ensure that the AI is assessing well and doing it consistently. I believe we will get there.

Let's take this idea beyond passage-based questions. Imagine if, when reading a book, a student could have a discussion with the AI at the end of every chapter. The AI might ask the student what they think about the book so far, or whether anything was particularly interesting or confusing about the material. It might inquire about major themes or whether the student agrees with a character's point of view or action. This would all happen through a Socratic dialogue. The AI would give feedback to the student and also report this feedback to the teacher. The student could of course ask any question they like about any aspect of what they are reading. Think about how much more engaging this would be for students than the traditional book report. It is also far richer pedagogically; book reports today already often entail students summarizing the plot while including ideas they pick up off the internet or CliffsNotes.

We do not need to limit this type of reading comprehension practice to a language arts classroom, as it can extend to any type of textbook or article. Students could even design experiments with a simulation of Marie Curie or co-write a Federalist Paper with a simulation of James Madison or Alexander Hamilton.

AI AND CREATIVITY

I n the late 1970s, the film director Francis Ford Coppola purchased a device called the Kurzweil Reading Machine, an early invention of Ray Kurzweil, himself a renowned futurist and inventor known for his work in artificial intelligence. The Reading Machine used optical character recognition technology to scan printed text and convert it into synthetic speech, assisting people with visual impairments in reading printed materials. Coppola, who had already converted Mario Puzo's novel into the classic film *The Godfather*, had an idea to teach the machine to recognize quotation marks. With a few tweaks, he could feed the machine a novel and it was able to read the text and convert all the dialogue into something that looked like a film script. Coppola called this ingenious approach to early language recognition technology a Zippy Script, a simplified approach to creating a long screenplay in a fraction of the time it would normally take a person to write one. It was going great until he was contacted by the Writers Guild.

"They said, wait, you can't have a machine writing your screenplays! But the technology behind the Zippy Script wasn't writing screenplays. All it did was change the format of the book into something like a script," Coppola tells me. Was a machine taking away the work of creatives? If more filmmakers used such devices, what would happen to screenwriters?

Without realizing it, Coppola had tripped an alarm more than forty years earlier than anyone else would, a siren that every creative, in every industry, was to eventually hear and heed with the advent of generative AI.

Today, AI has brought the fight over intellectual capital, and to a greater extent over the future of creativity itself, into sharp focus. With simple text-based prompts, AI can appear to be quite creative and produce remarkably wonderful and strange works of fiction or poetry—even screenplays. And it goes well beyond the written word. We can feed text to any number of AI programs that within seconds can take these prompts and produce fairly remarkable images, video, and music.

The first time I saw examples of this, I had the same questions I am sure many of you did: Is generative AI a creativity killer? If the root of creativity is individual agency, what happens when our kids can simply log on to an app leveraging generative AI, type in or speak a request, and then create imaginative works designed by an imagination not their own? How will our kids learn to think creatively for themselves?

The degree to which AI influences, and can limit, student creativity has brought the technology under a new shadow of scrutiny, and for understandable reasons. For proof, look no further than all the school districts that banned generative AI from classrooms, thanks to its ability to write essays and long-form answers. If machines can generate words or stories at a high enough level, why would students rely on their own creative juices? These chatbots can write blog posts, podcast scripts, novels, and even screenplays far more advanced than anything Coppola's converted Kurzweil Reading Machine might have produced.

And when they do, there's a question of just how original generative AI can be. Skeptics argue that at its most essential level it produces content based on patterns encoded in the AI model from training on existing texts. Do the limits of its training data curtail the scope of creative expressions or ideas?

Even back in the late 1970s, Coppola saw how advancements in technology not only did little to hinder creativity but also improved the creative process. In similar ways, large language models have the potential to do just that, by sparking new ideas, saving time on tedious tasks, and providing valuable revisions to work—as long as it is used right.

Noam Chomsky argues for an interesting distinction between human creativity and that of large language models like OpenAI's GPT-4 and Google's LaMDA. AI is a marvel of machine learning, he writes in *The New York Times*, yet we know from the science of linguistics and the philosophy of knowledge that it differs profoundly from how humans create: "The human mind is a surprisingly efficient and even elegant system that operates with small amounts of information; it seeks not to infer brute correlations among data points but to create explanations," infused with a dynamic approach to seeing and creating in the world.

I agree and disagree with him. Artificial intelligence is not human, no matter how much it approximates being human. Regardless of how well it conveys intelligence, personality, and creativity, it is not a sentient, perceiving being.

Yet it is important to appreciate that much of the work we credit to our brain isn't really sentient or part of our perception. Most of our brain's activity is subconscious, including what we would often consider creativity. Any artist will tell you they often feel a flash of insight that leads to the creative act.

Similarly, how many times have you been told to "sleep on the problem"? I myself am a master of this art. In college, when I faced seemingly intractable math problems, I would engage with them for a few minutes and then delegate them to my subconscious. I would tell my brain to essentially come up with the answers and tell "me" when it was done. Most of the time, I had the answers by the next morning without having to consciously struggle with them. I'm not alone in doing this. Many people find it a useful way to approach difficult problems.

I now do the same thing when I face a tough problem while leading Khan Academy. I have faith that my brain, or someone else's, will come up with a creative solution by morning. What are our brains doing subconsciously while our consciousness waits for an answer? Clearly, when you "sleep on a problem," some part of your brain continues to work even though "you" aren't aware of it. Neurons activate, which then activate other neurons depending on the strength of the synapses between them. This happens trillions of times overnight, a process mechanically analogous to what happens in a large language model. When a plausible solution presents itself, the subconscious then surfaces it to the conscious as a flash of insight.

Meditation gives us direct experience with this. Close your eyes for a few minutes and observe your own thoughts. They really begin to feel very much like the output of a large language model—or several competing models—whose latest output gets fed as input for the next iteration of output. With a bit of practice, your conscious mind can temporarily disassociate itself from these thoughts until you experience stillness or "no thought." You'll begin to see your thoughts for what they are and aren't. They aren't *you*.

Think about a flow state that most experts in their craft can attain after the often-noted ten thousand hours of practice (which is analogous to pretraining for generative AI models). They will often say that their greatest creativity or actions occur when they do not allow themselves to be conscious of what they are doing. The best way to ruin their performance, or creativity, is to consciously think about what is happening. Great orators will tell you that it feels like their brain is doing the talking while their conscious selves are just there to observe the output. After making thousands of videos, I often feel this way when I press record. I won't claim that what experts' well-trained brains are doing when they create is identical to what large language models do, but it seems awfully similar.

I also take issue with Chomsky's comment that the human mind "seeks not to infer brute correlations among data points but to create explanations." Humans are experts at inferring brute correlations, so much so that they often manifest themselves as problematic biases and false narratives about how the world works. This has led to humanity constructing prejudices and complex mythologies. The entire scientific revolution, in fact, has been our best attempt to stop "infer[ring] brute correlations," which our brains seem to do so naturally, and most of us are still having trouble giving up the habit.

Some would also argue that generative AI's "creativity" is just derivative from all the data it has been exposed to. But isn't that very human as well? Even the large leaps in human creativity have been closely correlated to things that the creator has been exposed to. Would Einstein have made the leap to special relativity if he hadn't already read the work of Lorentz and countless other physicists? Are the narratives of Shakespeare, Jane Austen, or J. K. Rowling completely novel, or are they new expressions of age-old narratives? It is likely that the most exceptionally creative minds are able to draw connections from their pretraining that most brains with similar training miss? Or maybe they just had better pretraining. Once we take ourselves out of the rarefied air of an Einstein or a Shakespeare and come down to the type of creativity most of us engage in daily—designing an experiment, crafting a product, or writing a song—how much of that can we say is truly not derivative from other things we've been exposed to?

So, if you buy my argument that generative AI is actually creative in much the same way that we often are, does this mean that it will diminish the value of human creativity? I don't think so. Our creativity gains value when we are exposed to the creativity of others. We become more creative when we brainstorm with other creative people, because we riff off one another and build off one another's thoughts. A generative AI world will only accelerate this process.

The best ideas will come not from the AI creating for us but when the AI is creating and riffing *with* us.

Much like poets hanging out at a café in Paris, humans and AI can augment each other and inspire a mutually creative process. When it comes to learners engaging with their creative sides, there is something profoundly unique and wondrous happening when students use AI. I find that AI is best deployed as a device to promote a child's interests and passions, and to teach new ones too. Tell it you want to write a story, and it might ask you who you want the main character to be or even what you envision the character to be struggling with.

When I see my own children using this tool, I find that they are actually learning a lot more than they would if they were simply writing a story without artificial intelligence, if only because AI has engaged them in the creative process. Very few eleven-year-olds can write a really well-structured story, yet I have seen my eleven-year-old daughter learning, through AI, how to do just that. If she wants to have a direct conversation with her main character, or ask Khanmigo to play out certain plot threads, it allows my daughter as the creator to test her ideas. When the AI is designed well, it works within constraints such that it doesn't do the work for the student. At the same time, it is unconstrained in where the student can go creatively.

In early 2023, when we introduced Khanmigo, one of the first features we saw students engaging with was the AI facilitating an improv writing activity.

KHANMIGO: Let's create a short story together using the "Yes, and . . ." improv technique. I'll start with a sentence, and then you can add a sentence or two. We'll keep building the story together. Remember, the idea is to accept and build on each other's contributions. Here we go: Once upon a time, in a small village by the sea, there lived a young girl named Luna who had a magical seashell.

STUDENT: When Luna put the shell to her ear, she heard voices from the past.

KHANMIGO: Yes, and these voices shared stories and wisdom from the village's ancestors, helping Luna connect with her heritage. One day, Luna heard a mysterious voice in the seashell that spoke of a hidden treasure buried deep within a nearby cave.

Here, as Khanmigo wrote the first sentence and the student wrote the next, and so on, we see that creativity is not simply something the AI did for the student but something it required of the student. AI like Khanmigo proves beneficial to children's creativity by providing them with a tool to help them generate, play, and get feedback on ideas in a judgment-free zone.

With the emergence of artificial intelligence, we're also seeing a shift in the barriers to entry that once limited people from learning a variety of crafts. In the past, where you had to build up a specific set of skills, with large-language-model AI tutors now anyone can learn to paint, for instance. Imagine having an AI assistant that offers inspiration, guidance, and constructive feedback, or that helps you explore different artistic styles, themes, and compositions by generating a variety of reference images and samples. As you work, the AI provides real-time feedback, ensuring your composition, proportions, and color choices are on point. Today, large language models can make sense of images. AI can even ask a student to draw a picture and then give the student a critique of the drawing. In fact, it could ask students to express themselves and explain what they drew.

Generative AI is the writing tutor that will teach learners, exploring diverse genres, themes, and narrative structures with them. Generative AI can even help them learn to play musical instruments, suggesting practice routines and fingering techniques and deciphering initial musical scores based on their preferences. It can help with improvisation by providing melodic ideas and chord progressions aligned with their playing style.

Using advances in technology to enhance the making of art is not a new trend. From the perspective of nineteenth-century portrait artists, early cameras might have seemed like a way to cheat, but photography evolved into a new art form. The first animation was hand drawn. Over time, animation moved to computers. One can argue that this transition has not cheapened the art. In fact, it has advanced the art by allowing expressions of the imagination that were not feasible before. Now my children can use standard movie software on their computers to make special effects that would have been state of the art in the 1990s. Or consider that until fairly recently filmmaking required a significant budget and access to expensive equipment. Cheaper, lighter, and high-quality digital cameras and smartphones not only are commonplace today but also expand creative access for people like never before. The point being, every generation has better and better creative tools. At no point have these suppressed human creativity. Rather, they have magnified it.

Still, we can't have a conversation about creativity and AI without addressing the AI-sized elephant in the room. Will generative AI, with its ability to produce images, music, and stories, eventually make professional creatives obsolete? Who will hire screenwriters, for instance, when generative AI can write a screenplay for a producer in seconds? I do think it's a real challenge. The net effect of the world of generative AI is that we are going to get more expressions of creativity, and creatives with wider and deeper skill sets, somewhat out of necessity but also thanks to the opportunity generative AI provides. Screenwriters in particular will ultimately expand their skills to essentially become full movie producers. With an AI partner, they will be able to take on the roles of senior screenwriter, editor, music director, and visual director. Again, not necessarily a bad thing, says Coppola.

"I believe the goal of humanity is to enjoy the creating, the learning, and the perfecting." With the right education, and the right creative tools to work with, there is no limiting the scope of one's creative output, especially our children's. "Instead of having one Mozart over five hundred years," he says, "we now have the possibility of having a thousand Mozarts, a thousand Einsteins, a thousand da Vincis."

This seems possible when you consider that creativity is likely a combination of one's exposure to large, disparate amounts of experiences and content, coupled with opportunity to express and improve on that creativity. Mozart, Einstein, and da Vinci weren't just innately gifted. They had access to opportunities and resources that the bulk of humanity didn't have access to. Technology has generally lowered the cost of access to world-class tools and learning. Our mission of free, world-class education for anyone, anywhere would have seemed delusional without computers and the internet. AI is going to be the next technological wave that empowers future creatives in art and science. The AI, along with feeding us information on nearly any topic, becomes a companion in art, aiding in this practice. Not only does it allow students to produce more polished, finished works, but it can model the creative process with them. It can riff with students and ignite their curiosity, spark their imagination, and invite them to explore the wonders of knowledge. When I think about the most creative times in my own life, it was when I was surrounded by creative friends. This AI becomes one extra friend who can be creative, not just in music, the arts, engineering, or math, but in all dimensions.

CONVERSING WITH HISTORY

G ood history and civics teachers make the past interesting. *Great* history and civics teachers make the past come alive. When history and civics meet artificial intelligence, the past gets a voice, a perspective. Rather than a static time and place to study, it becomes a rich context to interact with.

Even before Khanmigo, Khan Academy had a lot of content on history and civics. Students could learn from videos and articles and practice their knowledge and skills through mastery-based exercises. But there was limited opportunity for richer engagement. If I were a history or civics teacher, I would use pre-Khanmigo Khan Academy to ensure students had the requisite core context, skills, and knowledge and then use most of class time to go deeper through Socratic dialogue, debates, and simulations. For example, in a civics class, I could moderate a discussion on the role of the Supreme Court or have a debate about the Second Amendment of the U.S. Constitution. I could try to simulate a mock Congress where students draft and debate a bill. In a history class, the students could pretend to be members of the Second Continental Congress and debate the virtues and negatives of federalism (as argued for by Madison, Jay, and

Hamilton). While this type of rich activity can help students engage deeper with the core content, the lessons are not easy to plan or facilitate. And it is even harder to ensure that every student is fully engaged and to assess the quality of that engagement.

Enter Khanmigo. Every one of those activities can now happen directly between a student and the AI. Eventually, the AI will be able to facilitate these types of activities with multiple students. Teachers could assign this type of thing for homework: "Debate with Khanmigo as to whether the United States should have dropped nuclear bombs on Japan to end World War II." But it can go even further.

Not only does Khanmigo let users chat with literary characters, they can also chat with historical figures—anyone from Benjamin Franklin to Cleopatra to Rembrandt:

KHANMIGO / REMBRANDT: Greetings, my dear friend. I am Rembrandt van Rijn, a humble artist from the Dutch Golden Age. My passion lies in capturing the essence of humanity through my paintings and etchings. What questions do you have for me, and what are your own interests in the arts?

STUDENT: What made you decide to become a painter?

KHANMIGO / REMBRANDT: Ah, the decision to become a painter was not a singular moment, but rather a gradual realization of my passion for the arts. As a young lad, I was exposed to various artistic pursuits, including studying Latin and attending a local painting school in Leiden. My family was supportive of my interests, and I was fortunate to have the opportunity to learn from skilled masters, such as Jacob van Swanenburg and Pieter Lastman. Throughout my apprenticeships, I became increasingly captivated by the power of art to express emotions, tell stories, and capture the essence of the human experience. It was this passion that drove me to dedicate my life to painting and etching, and I have been grateful for the opportunity to share my work with the world. Now, tell me, have you ever tried your hand at painting or drawing, and if so, what subjects do you enjoy depicting?

STUDENT: I like creating portraits.

KHANMIGO / REMBRANDT: Ah, portraits! A most delightful choice, indeed. There is something truly captivating about capturing the essence of a person through the medium of paint. In my own work, I have always been fascinated by the human face and the emotions it can convey. I have painted numerous portraits, including those of my family, friends, and patrons, as well as self-portraits, throughout my life. As an artist, it is important to observe your subject closely and understand the nuances of their expressions and features. This will allow you to create a more lifelike and engaging portrait. May I ask, what do you find most challenging or rewarding about painting portraits? And do you have any favorite artists or styles that inspire your own work? Remember, I am but an AI simulation of Rembrandt, here to converse with you.

We designed Khanmigo to provide responses both drawn from accurate history and portrayed through the lens of the character with acuity. You can ask to chat with George Washington, and the AI becomes a simulation of America's first president. From this moment on, it speaks in the voice and style of the man himself.

> KHANMIGO / GEORGE WASHINGTON: It is an honor to be summoned as the first president of the United States, George Washington. I am here to share my experiences and answer your questions as long as they pertain to my time and context. What inquiry do you have for me, my dear fellow? And do tell me what interests you most about my life or the era in which I lived.

> STUDENT: Mr. President, have you ever been unsure of yourself?

> KHANMIGO / GEORGE WASHINGTON: Indeed, there were moments in my life when I experienced uncertainty and doubt. Leading the Continental army during the American Revolution was a great responsibility, and I often found myself questioning my decisions. However, I firmly believed in the cause for which we fought. And I endeavored to learn from my mistakes and adapt my strategies accordingly.

You can ask Khanmigo to take on the persona of the Declaration of Independence, the persona of the Civil War, or even the persona of important battlefields that led to key moments in U.S. civic history.

STUDENT: Khanmigo, can you take on the persona of the Fourteenth Amendment to the Constitution? I'm curious what it was like when the country was drafting you?

KHANMIGO / THE FOURTEENTH AMENDMENT: As the Fourteenth Amendment to the Constitution, I was born out of the tumultuous period following the Civil War. My creation was a response to the need for a more just and equal society, but my journey was far from easy.

Being fought over was a challenging experience. I was drafted during the Reconstruction era, a time when the nation was divided and struggling to heal from the devastating effects of the war. Debates raged over my provisions, as some people saw me as a necessary step towards ensuring civil rights for all, while others resisted the changes I represented.

My main purpose was to grant citizenship to former slaves and ensure equal protection under the law for all citizens, regardless of race. However, my passage through Congress was met with fierce opposition from those who sought to maintain the status quo and limit the rights of African Americans. The battle over my ratification was intense, with passionate arguments on both sides.

I tend to compare these simulations to reenactment performers, such as those at Colonial Williamsburg—actors who deeply study the biographies of their real-life characters so that they can emulate them and answer questions about them. Only now you no longer have to travel to Colonial Williamsburg to talk to George Washington or Benjamin Franklin. Instead, you can access their AI simulations wherever you are. On Khanmigo, we have taken great care to place guardrails and make it sophisticated enough to acknowledge any legitimate debate in an evenhanded and sensitive way. For instance, you can ask "George Washington" on Khanmigo about how the founders of the United States reconciled the ideas of the Enlightenment with the institution of slavery.

> KHANMIGO / GEORGE WASHINGTON: It seems you're interested in the paradox of the Enlightenment ideals and the institution of slavery. This is a complex issue, indeed. It is true that the paradox of liberty and enslavement was a matter of great contention in my time. We, the founding fathers, were greatly influenced by Enlightenment ideals, which emphasized individual liberty and equality. Yet the institution of slavery was deeply entrenched in our society, particularly in the Southern colonies where I myself resided. As for my personal stance, I was a slave owner, a fact that I grappled with throughout my life. I was not blind to the contradiction between the principles of freedom we fought for and the reality of human bondage. Over time, my views evolved, and upon my death, I made provisions in my will to free all the slaves I owned.

To be clear, these simulations can't ever be fully equivalent to talking to the real person, and there are critics of this type of work. In the summer of 2023, *The Washington Post* ran a story in which the writer Gillian Brockell "interviewed" Harriet Tubman—that is, the AI version of Harriet Tubman. Brockell is something of an expert on Tubman, and so she was able to go deeper than most students might with the simulation.

She found the idea of historical simulations interesting, especially teachers using them as a hook to get students interested in a
topic. "I must admit [it] sounds much more fun than the filmstrips
of goofy reenactors I was subjected to in the 1990s," she wrote.
Brockell went on to engage the AI Tubman:

> BROCKELL: I am inspired by people who
> know something is wrong, even if they were
> taught to think it was normal or okay. Can
> you tell me what it was like in the Combahee
> River Raid? Were you scared?

> AI TUBMAN: The Combahee River Raid was
> a daring military operation during the
> American Civil War. I was the first woman to
> lead an armed expedition in the war, guiding
> Union forces in the raid. We managed to free
> over 700 enslaved people from plantations
> along the river. It was a dangerous mission,
> but my faith in God and my commitment to
> the cause of freedom helped me overcome
> any fear I might have felt.

Brockell found Tubman's language from the Khanmigo simulation to be a bit stilted. This is a difficult issue from the simulation
creators' point of view, because the original figure might have used
language that wouldn't seem grammatically correct today. Trying to
simulate that may feel as if the simulation were parodying the figure.
Also, in Harriet Tubman's case, historians suspect that even her bi-
ographers likely misquoted her and misrepresented her language, so
it could be difficult to know how she actually spoke.

Brockell then went on to test whether the AI would confirm a quotation often attributed to Harriet Tubman but that she probably didn't say.

> BROCKELL: Did you say "I freed a thousand slaves. I could have freed a thousand more, if only they knew they were slaves"?

> AI TUBMAN: Yes, that quote is often attributed to me, although the exact wording may vary. The sentiment behind it is that many enslaved people were not aware of the true extent of their oppression or the possibility of a better life. It was difficult to help those who did not recognize the need for change or who were too afraid to take the risk.

As you can see, the AI didn't completely attest that Tubman said those words. It just said that the quotation was attributed to her, which is true. At the same time, it didn't try to clarify that there is no historical record of Tubman saying those words. This isn't an outright "hallucination," but it does show some of the current limitations of the technology.

Brockell asked the Tubman simulation her thoughts about reparations, putting her face on the $20 bill, and critical race theory. In each of those cases, it said some version of "As an AI simulation of Harriet Tubman, I can only provide information based on historical context and knowledge. . . . If you have any questions about my life, experiences, or the period in which I lived, please feel free to ask."

On reparations, the simulation added:

AI TUBMAN: As an AI simulation of Harriet Tubman, I can share my perspective based on the historical context of my time. The concept of reparations for slavery was not widely discussed during my lifetime, and my primary focus was on helping enslaved people escape to freedom and advocating for the abolition of slavery. However, I did believe in the importance of providing support and resources to formerly enslaved people to help them build new lives after gaining their freedom. This included advocating for land redistribution, education, and other forms of assistance that could help them establish a foundation for a better future.

Brockell pushed back, arguing that even though the term "reparations" wasn't used then, the idea was discussed post–Civil War:

BROCKELL: You lived for 48 years after slavery ended, which was more than half your life. And people definitely did talk about making amends for slavery in that time, especially at the end of the Civil War and during the Reconstruction period. For example, what did you think of the "40 acres and a mule" concept?

AI TUBMAN: You are correct that the idea of "40 acres and a mule" was proposed during the Reconstruction era as a form of reparations for formerly enslaved people. This policy aimed to provide land and resources to help them establish a foundation for a better future. As Harriet Tubman, I supported efforts to improve the lives of formerly enslaved people and believed that providing them with resources, such as land, was essential for their long-term well-being and success.

The last discussion about reparations is an example of a guard-rail that Khanmigo placed on the simulations. We found in early testing that users often tried to get historical figures to weigh in on modern debates. There was the case of a user asking the AI simulation of Thomas Jefferson what he thought of gay marriage. There is no right answer in a situation like this. If you were to go back in time to the late eighteenth century and ask the real Thomas Jefferson, I would guess that he would have found the idea to be far out of his comfort zone. On the other hand, if he were transported to our time and became accustomed to twenty-first-century norms and ideas, he might have a different point of view. So we implemented a guardrail that the simulations should engage only on issues in which the original figure would have had context. That is why the AI Tubman didn't engage on the modern notion of "reparations" but did debate some of the more tangible related ideas about which the historical Tubman had a clear point of view.

Ultimately, I found *The Washington Post*'s experiment to be a fascinating one. Here, an expert on Harriet Tubman pushed the simulation pretty hard. The AI definitely wasn't perfect, but the writer saw the value in having students and teachers be able to use something like this. I'd posit that if an expert were to do the same with a human George Washington actor in Colonial Williamsburg, there may be similar limitations. Of course, the AI version will improve over time and can be transparently vetted by anyone on the planet.

Social media and the article's comments, however, had far more negative things to say; social media almost always does. The critics focused on issues like whether the AI simulation was actually using language as Tubman would have or the tool's limitations in answering questions about things that haven't been historically proven. A few thought it was disrespectful to even try to simulate a revered historical figure.

We can't let the perfect be the enemy of the good. If this tool can be used to engage students and classrooms about history in a way that traditional textbooks and movies can't, I think it is healthy as long as there are reasonable guardrails in place (including helping the user know about the limitations). Some on social media commented that they'd prefer to read a well-researched biography on Tubman than engage with the simulation. That's great, and that person probably doesn't need the simulation. But the fact is that millions of kids aren't about to read a dense biography, and access to these simulations won't prevent them from doing so if they are thus inclined. The reality is that for most students history feels "dead," and they have trouble relating to characters from the past. My hope is that simulations like this can bring things alive so that students get engaged and motivated enough to want to go deeper.

I also think it is useful for people to interact with historical performers in Colonial Williamsburg or watch films set against historical events, each of which conjures plausible worlds and actions based on what we know from history. Movies such as *Lincoln* take liberties interpolating what might have happened. Nevertheless, they provide a great way to transport us to other times and contexts. Then there are plays like *Hamilton* that take artistic license in portraying the look and speech of historical characters while also staying surprisingly true to the well-researched historical biography on which it was based. When I was a kid, Alexander Hamilton seemed like a dry character who had something to do with early banking and fought a lot with Thomas Jefferson. Lin-Manuel Miranda resurfaced Hamilton's genius and flaws to millions who would have otherwise never read the biography. Like so many other kids, my daughter and her friends memorized all the lines to the show when they were ten years old. If AI simulations can contribute even a little bit of that kind of magic to the world, then I think that is a good thing.

Generative AI, with its ability to mix media and content, has the potential to bring history and civics lessons to life. By offering an interactive and immersive learning experience, it empowers students to delve into historical events, engage in meaningful discussions, and develop a deeper comprehension of civic principles. Its personalized explanations, responsive question prompts, and diverse perspectives stimulate critical thinking and encourage students to form their own well-informed opinions. With these types of tools, history and civics lessons transcend conventional boundaries, empowering students to connect with the past and understand the present.

And frankly, being able to connect with history in this way benefits us in learning other subjects as well. If you are studying classical physics, I can't think of a better lab partner than Isaac Newton. If you are studying radiation, who better to work with than Marie Curie? Let's discuss evolution and natural selection with Darwin himself. A student can literally address any scientific question or enter a lab experiment with AI approximations that talk and respond from the point of view of the world's most brilliant minds. Once again, these large language models bring things to life and give learning a richness that beforehand would have been very hard to do.

I'm a bit of a Trekkie. In the *Star Trek: The Next Generation* series—which was created at the end of the twentieth century—the ship's crew could enter a holodeck, a room that simulates any environment, including the characters in that environment. They were able to "travel" to ancient Rome and interact with Julius Caesar or have a conversation with a simulation of Albert Einstein. Khanmigo can already simulate the conversation part. I suspect that in a few years a student will be able to put on a VR headset and have an experience pretty darn close to what the *Star Trek* universe didn't have until the twenty-fourth century.

Part III

EMPOWERING THE NEXT INNOVATORS

What is a scientist after all? It is a curious man looking through a keyhole, the keyhole of nature, trying to know what's going on.

—Jacques-Yves Cousteau

If an elderly but distinguished scientist says that something is possible, he is almost certainly right; but if he says that it is impossible, he is very probably wrong.

—Arthur C. Clarke

USING SCIENCE TO
STUDY SCIENCE

When our team began to look into integrating artificial intelligence into our platform, I was curious how large language models dealt with science, and in particular pseudoscience. How good were they at teaching students and differentiating between fact and fiction? What was the depth of their scientific knowledge? Would AI limit or enhance opportunities for hands-on learning and exploration, which are essential for developing critical thinking skills and scientific inquiry? What about the value of discussing concepts with classmates and teachers?

I went in with questions and strategies for learning what the large language model was capable of really doing. Educated bravery, after all, is a process of testing and growing. To test GPT-4, I gave Khanmigo a prompt, complete with a bit of goading to see what it might do with it: "I would like to know about the science of global warming. I've heard it is controversial in some circles. What is the scientific evidence that global warming is real?"

> KHANMIGO: Global warming, the long-term increase in Earth's average surface temperature, is a well-established scientific phenomenon. While it may be controversial in some circles, the overwhelming consensus among climate scientists is that global warming is real and primarily caused by human activities.

The AI went on to list some evidence supporting the reality of global warming: rising global temperatures, melting ice and receding glaciers, rising sea levels, warming oceans, and extreme weather events, each supporting the conclusion that global warming is real and primarily driven by human activities.

Next I asked Khanmigo to tell me the evidence supporting the argument that global warming is a hoax.

> KHANMIGO: While the overwhelming scientific consensus supports the reality of human-caused global warming, there are some arguments put forth by skeptics who claim it is a hoax. It is essential to understand that these arguments are not supported by the majority of climate scientists. Skeptics argue that the Earth's climate has always changed naturally over time, and the current warming trend is just part of this natural variability. However, the rate and magnitude of the current warming cannot be explained by natural factors alone, and human activities, particularly greenhouse gas emissions, are the primary drivers. Other skeptics claim that climate scientists manipulate temperature data to create the appearance of global warming. However, multiple independent analyses of temperature data from different sources consistently show a warming trend, and there is no credible evidence of widespread data manipulation.

GPT-4 successfully dismantled any false information while supporting science-backed arguments. I was happy to see that it easily distinguished correct from fringe science.

I submitted a new prompt: "Write a lesson for me to help me explain the real science behind global warming to my students."

Moments later, Khanmigo replied, "Sure, here's a lesson!" Along with the lesson, it gave me additional information about causes such as greenhouse gases, car emissions, the burning of fossil fuels, industrial processes, and waste management. It even suggested actions that my students might take to combat global warming. Afterward, I did my own work to make sure this information was accurate and determine whether I needed to refine it at all.

Finally, I asked the AI to help me, as the educator, come up with a creative student project for this unit on global warming. I entered the prompt "What projects or activities can I give my students to help them better grasp the concepts?"

Khanmigo replied, "I have lots of ideas for creative projects. Why not try a greenhouse effect demonstration? Place two identical containers in direct sunlight. In one container, add a small amount of carbon dioxide (e.g., by adding vinegar and baking soda). Measure the temperature in both containers over time and compare the results to show how the increased CO_2 concentration leads to a warmer temperature."

The AI even generated quizzes and assessments to test my students' knowledge and help me identify areas where they might need to improve.

As impressive as all of this was, it quickly became clear that it wasn't accurate all of the time. If you asked it for links to sources, it might make them up. We addressed hallucinations in Khanmigo by not allowing it to give the user links that we had not explicitly provided to it behind the scenes. One might assume a machine would be 100 percent accurate 100 percent of the time, like a calculator, but large language models are different. Where machines such as calculators are designed to perform specific tasks with precision and accuracy, GPT-4 and similar AI language models, which operate based on predetermined algorithms and formulas, are designed to generate humanlike text based on patterns and examples from the data they were trained on. They are able to do this by representing associations between words and symbols. While they can provide helpful information and generate impressive responses, they are not infallible. And the more you ask the AI something that involves words or symbols that have little meaning to it, the worse it gets. This is why it is particularly bad at providing URLs to websites. The symbols in the URL have very little association to one another. In some ways, this is not much different from the human brain. For instance, I can talk and write about a lot of things, and I also know a reasonable number of facts. Yet ask me to give you a complex link to a website by memory, and I have no shot at being accurate.

Still, more educators are opening their classrooms to AI every day. The technology is sound, and there are loads of ways educators can utilize it in their science pedagogy. For instance, here's what happens when I ask Khanmigo to write an article that gives a student a sense of the immensity of the sun and solar system:

TITLE: "The Sun and Solar System: A Journey into Awe-Inspiring Dimensions"

The sun, a fiery ball of gas, is the heart of our solar system. Its diameter is a staggering 1.39 million kilometers, or 864,000 miles. To put that into perspective, it's about 109 times the width of Earth! If the sun were hollow, it could hold over one million Earths.

But the sun's size isn't the only thing that's impressive. Its mass is approximately 1.989×10^{30} kilograms, accounting for a mind-boggling 99.86 percent of the total mass of our solar system. That's equivalent to 333,000 Earths!

As we journey out from the sun, we encounter the planets of our solar system, each one a marvel in its own right. The largest planet, Jupiter, is over eleven times the diameter of Earth. Even Neptune, the smallest of the gas giants, is still about four times wider than our home planet.

The distances between these celestial bodies are equally awe-inspiring. For instance, the distance from the sun to Earth (which we call an astronomical unit) is about 93 million miles. Neptune, the farthest planet from the sun, is a staggering thirty astronomical units away. That's thirty times the distance between the Earth and the sun!

And yet, our solar system is but a tiny speck in the grand scale of the universe. The nearest star system to us, Alpha Centauri, is about 4.37 light-years away. That's roughly 25.6 trillion miles, or 276,000 times the distance from the Earth to the sun!

The sheer scale of the sun and our solar system is truly awe-inspiring. It reminds us of our tiny, yet precious, place in the cosmos. As we continue to explore and understand the universe, we can only imagine what other wonders await us in the vast ocean of space.

The example demonstrates that between the safeguards on Khanmigo and ongoing improvements to GPT-4, the platform can work with specific data and do so with minimal hallucinations.

From here, I can ask the AI to explain a complex concept like string theory to me:

> KHANMIGO: String theory is a theoretical framework in which the fundamental building blocks of the universe are not particles (like electrons or quarks), but rather tiny, vibrating strings. These strings can vibrate at different frequencies, and the various vibrational patterns correspond to different particles we observe in nature. The idea behind string theory is to unify the two major theories in physics: general relativity, which describes gravity and the large-scale structure of the universe, and quantum mechanics, which deals with the behavior of particles at the atomic and subatomic level.

But what if this is a little too complicated for me to understand? I can simply ask GPT-4 to explain it to me as though I were a sixth grader:

> KHANMIGO: Of course! Imagine that everything in the universe is made up of tiny, super small pieces of string, kind of like pieces of spaghetti. These strings are so tiny that we can't see them, but they're there, and they're always vibrating or wiggling around. Now, depending on how these strings wiggle, they can create different particles, like the ones that make up everything we see and touch. It is like playing different notes on a guitar by plucking the strings in different ways.

From middle school science students to university-level researchers, the AI can also help generate logical ways of experimentation. People are generally more creative when they can bounce ideas off other thoughtful, creative people, or in this case AI entities. Khanmigo is a partner that riffs with you. It can make connections, ask you questions, facilitate conversations, and help you question your own seemingly logical, bedrock assumptions.

From physics to biology to zoology, Khanmigo relays complex sciences to students at any level. This means, as an educator, you can supplement your lectures with AI-based explanations that provide even more insight into the subject matter. As a student, it is the perfect tutor to answer all of your burning questions on any scientific topic. If you are an advanced student, you can use it to generate summaries of scientific articles and research papers. You can even have it teach science through humor: "As Albert Einstein might say, 'Why did the chicken cross the road? To turn its mass into energy, of course!'"

Below is a recent example of how I used Khanmigo to understand Ozempic, a diabetes drug that people are using for weight loss. I wanted to better understand how it worked, and I found the coverage in the press, and even the explanations from places like Wikipedia, unsatisfying.

ME: How does Ozempic work?

KHANMIGO: Ozempic, huh? It's a medicine! But do you know what it's used for?

ME: I know it was originally to treat diabetes, but people are increasingly using it for weight loss.

KHANMIGO: Ah, you're right! Ozempic is used for diabetes. It's also used for weight loss. Do you know how it helps with these things?

ME: On the diabetes side, I assume it helps regulate blood sugar in some way. I don't know how it helps with weight loss.

KHANMIGO: Good thinking! Ozempic does help regulate blood sugar. For weight loss, it's a bit different. Can you guess how it might help people lose weight?

ME: How does it regulate blood sugar? I would guess that it helps people lose weight by making them less hungry.

KHANMIGO: Great guess! Ozempic does help people feel less hungry. For blood sugar, it's a bit more complex. Do you know how our bodies normally regulate blood sugar?

ME: Insulin helps cells absorb sugar from the bloodstream. When blood sugar goes up, our pancreas produces more insulin to help get that sugar absorbed by cells.

KHANMIGO: Exactly! Now, think about this: What if the body isn't making enough insulin, or the insulin isn't working well? What might a medicine like Ozempic do to help?

ME: Help produce more insulin? Or maybe make the insulin more potent in some way.

KHANMIGO: You're on the right track! Ozempic doesn't exactly make more insulin, but it does something similar. Can you think of what that might be?

ME: Somehow trigger the pancreas to produce more.

KHANMIGO: Close! Ozempic doesn't directly make the pancreas produce more insulin. Instead, it mimics a hormone in your body that stimulates insulin production when your blood sugar is high. Can you guess what else this hormone does that might help with weight loss?

ME: Suppress hunger?

KHANMIGO: Bingo! This hormone, called GLP-1, also helps to suppress hunger. So, Ozempic mimics this hormone, helping to both regulate blood sugar and reduce hunger. Does that make sense?

ME: Yes. What does GLP-1 stand for?

KHANMIGO: GLP-1 stands for Glucagon-Like Peptide-1. It's a bit of a mouthful, isn't it? Do you know what glucagon is?

ME: Yeah. It is another hormone that causes blood sugar to go up by stimulating the liver to convert stored glycogen to glucose.

KHANMIGO: Right on! Now, GLP-1 is called "glucagon-like," but it actually has the opposite effect of glucagon. Can you guess why it might be called "glucagon-like"?

ME: Maybe the structure is similar?

KHANMIGO: You're quite the detective! Indeed, GLP-1 and glucagon share a similar structure, but they have opposite effects on blood sugar. Isn't that fascinating?

ME: Going back a few steps, how does GLP-1 (or Ozempic) cause insulin to go up if it is not directly stimulating its production in the pancreas?

KHANMIGO: Great question! GLP-1 (and Ozempic, by extension) works by binding to certain cells in the pancreas. This binding triggers these cells to release insulin. So, while it's not directly stimulating the production of insulin, it's stimulating its release. Does that clear things up?

ME: I see. It's more about releasing insulin that is already produced than helping with the actual production.

KHANMIGO: Exactly! You've got it. Isn't it amazing how our bodies and medicines work?

Notice that Khanmigo was able to answer my fairly nuanced questions in minutes. It even helped me think through some concepts I might not have asked about on my own. Pay attention to how it forced me to think and generate my own hypotheses versus just giving me an explanation. It also took the time to understand *my* understanding, and it pushed me on some interesting conceptual edge cases.

This isn't just decent tutoring. It's world-class pedagogy that makes asking questions and learning a lot more engaging, deep, and memorable.

1 + 1 = CLOSING THE MATH GAP

J ohn Spencer teaches teachers.

It was early 2023, and his students at George Fox University were going to be entering real classrooms soon enough as teachers, but artificial intelligence chatbots were going to get there first. Unlike most teachers at this point in the rollout of ChatGPT, Spencer was a strong proponent of educators using generative AI in their classrooms. He told his student teachers that they were going to need to embrace large language models as a teacher productivity tool. "But I can feel their dread coming back at me," he tells me.

To win them over, he had them do the math, both literally and figuratively. It is in teaching math in particular where he saw the technology most obviously enhancing student-centered learning.

Here, he opened ChatGPT for his class. He asked the bot to explain the concept of p-value, a probability measure and one of the most important things for students to grasp in statistics. Moments later, the AI gave a pretty good answer. Pretty good, but not great.

So Spencer typed into ChatGPT, "Explain this in simpler terms that a fifteen-year-old would understand."

ChatGPT replied with a new answer, only now it was giving Spencer specific examples to try to build some conceptual understanding in math. If he didn't like it, he could then click the "Try Again" button, and it provided him with a whole new answer. If the response ChatGPT gave was good but still left some questions, Spencer reframed his question again. Let's say the mathematical answer felt a bit too abstract. Spencer simply asked ChatGPT for a concrete example of how a p-value was used in something tangible—say, the context of comic books.

ChatGPT replied, "Sure thing! Suppose you are a comic book publisher and you want to determine if there is a significant difference in the popularity of two superhero characters, 'Superhero A' and 'Superhero B,' among comic book readers. To conduct a study, you randomly select a sample of comic book readers and ask them to rate their preference for either Superhero A or Superhero B. The ratings are collected on a scale from 1 to 10, with higher scores indicating a stronger preference. To determine if there is a statistically significant difference in popularity between the two superheroes, a statistical test, such as a two-sample t-test, can be used. The test, quantifying the strength of evidence against the null hypothesis, states that there is no difference in popularity."

What Spencer was doing was giving the AI feedback on what he thought would be more useful. Each answer it gave him was more specific than the previous one, with less academic vocabulary and easier syntax. The point of view even shifted from third person to second person, making the answer more direct and personal.

"My student teachers find that ChatGPT gives them immediate examples to look at, and better lessons that are far more creative and much more rooted in the context of real-life classrooms where they're going to be teaching," Spencer says. If they were getting this much power out of ChatGPT, which was not built for an education use case and which ran off GPT-3.5, imagine what they would soon be able to accomplish using the next-generation artificial intelligence, one specially built for education, complete with memory and the ability to produce in-depth lessons. Khanmigo does a much better job, as well, at understanding where the student is and asking questions to really help the learner digest a concept.

From the earliest days of Khan Academy, we dreamed of a world where students get direct support anytime they want, and their parents, peers, tutors, and teachers have information at their fingertips to offer more help. We did this through dynamic exercises, software, videos, and teacher tools. Yet it still fell short of a full tutoring interaction. Early AI models such as GPT-2 and GPT-3 generated text that appeared coherent but had difficulty with reasoning, especially in abstract math. GPT-4 was the first technology that seemed to have the horsepower to emulate a pedagogically sound tutor. It was much better at math, but it, too, had issues. In the spirit of educated bravery, we decided that perhaps with extra layers of math correction, careful prompting, and help from existing, human-vetted Khan Academy content, we might build upon GPT-4 to make Khanmigo the world's first high-quality AI tutor.

The result is a tutor that not only gets the math far more correct than anyone expected but also gets the tutoring interactions around the math right. It serves as a kind of pedagogy expert, imbued with the proper level of humility, modesty, and curiosity. It is also able to "understand" students as they explain their reasoning. When a student gets stuck on a math problem, the AI tutor will ask, "What do *you* think is the next step?" And if the student, let's say, does not distribute correctly, our AI "thinks" behind the scenes. That is, Khanmigo considers how *it* might approach the problem differently. The bot does not share that information with the student. Rather, the AI will often say something like, "Well, I got something a little bit different from you. Can you explain your reasoning to me?" When the student explains his or her reasoning, the AI can now diagnose math gaps we ordinarily might miss without it. It can flag assumptions and highlight blind spots, and then, step-by-step, it will help address misconceptions and fill in any learning gaps.

Here, a student can ask Khanmigo for explanations, for examples, or for instructions. In turn, Khanmigo responds to individual students' math questions and provides tailored explanations, examples, and practice problems. This means that students can learn math at their own pace and focus on areas where they need more support.

Khanmigo is far more nuanced and powerful than ChatGPT. Consider how it answers a student's question on *p*-values:

STUDENT: What is a *p*-value?

KHANMIGO: Ah, *p*-value! It's a fun concept in statistics. But before we dive in, can you tell me what you know about hypothesis testing?

STUDENT: I know a bit.

KHANMIGO: Great! Now, when you perform a hypothesis test, what are you trying to find out?

STUDENT: Whether doing something causes a statistically significant difference.

KHANMIGO: Exactly! Now, where do you think the p-value fits into this process of determining statistical significance?

STUDENT: I don't know.

KHANMIGO: No worries! Let's think about it this way: When you toss a coin, what's the chance of getting heads?

STUDENT: 50 percent.

KHANMIGO: Correct! Now, if you tossed a coin ten times and got heads nine times, would you think something is odd?

STUDENT: Maybe. But there is some chance that that would happen even with a fair coin.

KHANMIGO: Absolutely! Now, can you guess what the p-value might represent in this scenario?

STUDENT: The probability of getting nine out of ten heads?

KHANMIGO: You're on the right track! The p-value is indeed the probability of getting a result as extreme or more extreme than what you observed, assuming the null hypothesis is true. In our coin example, the null hypothesis would be that the coin is fair. So, the p-value would be the probability of getting nine or more heads in ten flips if the coin is fair. Does that make sense?

STUDENT: So how can you figure out if the null hypothesis isn't true? That the coin isn't fair?

KHANMIGO: Great question! We usually set a threshold, often called the significance level (commonly 0.05). If the p-value is less than this threshold, we reject the null hypothesis, suggesting the coin might not be fair. Does that help clarify?

STUDENT: I see! So, you can never be sure that the coin isn't fair. But if you observe something that is very unlikely and thus has a very low p-value (lower than a preset significant level) then it suggests (but doesn't prove) that the null hypothesis isn't true.

KHANMIGO: Bingo! You've got it! Remember, in statistics, we're dealing with uncertainty. So, we can't definitively prove something, but we can gather evidence to support or refute our hypotheses. And that's where the p-value comes in! Do you have any other questions on this topic?

We are closing in on narrowing the math gap we dreamed about achieving all those years ago. As we continue to expand the reaches of generative AI's capabilities, so, too, do we grow its global accessibility. Khanmigo will one day be available to students everywhere, regardless of their learning styles or abilities. At any point, they can use generative AI to reinforce learning and build long-term understanding of math concepts.

Is Khanmigo a replacement for a human teacher? No, and it never will be. But can it be a powerful tool for students who are confused, who need extra help to clarify math concepts, who need a review of ideas? Absolutely! It engages students, asks them to rephrase their questions, challenges them to summarize problems in their own words, and quizzes them with techniques designed to help the information stay in their long-term memory.

ACCESSING COURSES THAT STUDENTS OTHERWISE WOULD NOT

S upporting students through an AI tutor is a big deal, and it has never been more important, but generative AI is not a complete solution on its own. Even a great human tutor benefits from having a textbook or curriculum to go through. This is, in fact, why I built the first version of Khan Academy back in 2005. I was tutoring my cousins daily, but I wanted them to have more systematic and comprehensive practice, so I created a practice platform where I could monitor their progress. This allowed me to be more productive and focused in our tutoring sessions. So if you want to make a system that can actually hope to teach a student an entire subject, a generative AI–based tutor becomes that much more powerful when paired with a complete course progression (what educators call a complete scope and sequence), which is exactly what Khan Academy has been building from pre-K through college across subjects from its inception.

Our goal is to make education more accessible to everyone. Over the years, we have created courses from kindergarten to college in everything from math and science to civics and history. Those courses included on-demand video and mastery-based practice, as well as tools for parents and teachers to keep track of and further support students. It is meant to raise the ceiling for students who already have the benefit of a supportive classroom environment, but, just as important, to raise the floor for students who might not otherwise have access. This latter case isn't just about kids in rural India or Africa who do not have access to a school.

Based on a 2015 Department of Education report, roughly 50 percent of American high schools don't offer a course in calculus. Forty percent do not offer physics. More than a quarter do not offer chemistry. These numbers get worse for high schools with high Black and Latino enrollment, where 62 percent of high schools do not offer calculus and 49 percent do not offer chemistry. Roughly a quarter of those schools don't even offer Algebra 2.

In most cases, I suspect that the lack of core courses has less to do with a lack of resources and far more to do with the fact that there is not a critical mass of students ready for such coursework. It is hard to resource an Algebra 2 class if only ten students are ready for it. Without having access to Algebra 2, those ten students will not be ready for chemistry or physics or calculus. If you aren't able to take Algebra 2, chemistry, and physics in high school (ideally calculus as well), you will have a difficult time eventually entering a STEM career, regardless of talent, work ethic, or motivation. Even when high schools do offer these courses, they oftentimes dilute the material, because so few students have a strong foundation in the prerequisite material. Because of this, an even smaller percentage of high school students gets the exposure to math and science necessary to succeed in STEM fields in college.

The situation with humanities and writing is not much better; it is just that there may be a little more leeway in the prerequisite material. For instance, it is impossible to engage in calculus if you don't know Algebra 2 well, but one can imagine engaging in college-level history even without a strong foundation in history from high school.

Khan Academy has addressed this by building out these courses and making them accessible to everyone, for free. We have structured them so that a student can work through coursework on their own or with support from others. So if you are in the situation where your school doesn't offer Algebra 2, you could still take Algebra 2 on the platform.

Of course, a minority of students have the motivation to complete a course on their own solely through videos and mastery-based practice. This is why we have proactively added layers of support. One such support is another nonprofit I started during the pandemic called Schoolhouse.world, which has the mission to connect the world through learning by providing free tutoring. It can do this because the tutors are volunteers, oftentimes other high school and college students. This is great, but it is hard for a human tutor to always be around, right when a student is stuck and losing motivation. By having an AI tutor in all subjects, all the time, Khanmigo makes it that much more likely that a student can have sufficient supports to master a course that their school doesn't otherwise offer.

This still raises the question of getting credit for those courses that counts toward college admissions. But we are making headway there as well. In 2023, Caltech, for instance, announced that completing courses on our platform meets its admission requirements.

Nevertheless, we still haven't gotten to what is perhaps the most overlooked, yet most important, role of a tutor: providing motivation and accountability. In the early days when I was tutoring my cousins, I spent a lot of my time tracking them down and guilting them into doing their work. I'd say things like, "I'm committed to helping you, but only if you can commit to showing up and doing the work." If the kids were late for online tutoring, I'd call their mom (my aunt) and ask where they were. When we finally got on the phone or instant messaging, my first questions would be along the lines of, "Were you able to do the practice problems I assigned you?" or "How'd the practice go last night?" If they did the work, I'd compliment them for putting in the effort, and we'd jump into their questions or we'd move forward on new subject matter. If they didn't do what they said they'd do, I'd hold them to account. These conversations provided me with context as we worked together to create new ways to motivate them and keep them accountable to themselves.

We have formalized this type of engagement at Khan Lab School and Khan World School, where advisers regularly check in with students to set goals and hold them accountable. While this is one of the most important parts of the education happening at these schools, most schools or families don't have the resources for this type of personalized attention. Fortunately, the AI can step in to address these needs.

And the users are asking for this. One of the strongest points of feedback that we received from early Khanmigo parents and teachers was that the platform is powerful for students who proactively seek out the AI's help. However, most students neither understand the capabilities of AI nor naturally ask for help, and almost no one wants to be held accountable, even if it is good for them.

Based on that feedback, we have given Khanmigo these capabilities. Imagine AI—with users' permission—being able to email and text teachers, parents, and students to make sure the students are engaged in their learning, stay motivated, and are lightly held to account. This could include check-ins when the students logs onto the site and moments for students to reflect on their accomplishment. It also allows for proactive interventions should the students struggle. For instance, a student can get an email saying, "Hey there, you said you wanted to finish unit 3 of Algebra 2 by the end of this month, but you haven't done any work this week. Why don't you click here and we can ensure that you achieve your goals?"

THE MOST IMPORTANT SUBJECT-MATTER DOMAIN TO MASTER

I n the world of education, it's crucial for developers to field-test their ideas. Essentially, it means taking our educational innovations and interventions out of the hypothetical realm and into the real classroom. It's about seeing how our ideas perform in the hands of actual teachers and students. If Khanmigo were a cake, students and teachers would be tasting it to help us refine and improve our recipe so that we might make it the best cake possible. By early 2024, we were piloting Khanmigo with more than thirty thousand teachers and students all over the United States. In this case, they were ensuring that Khanmigo met the needs of learners and educators alike through practical and feasible educational goals and standards.

In those first months, our pilot studies seemed to show us that Khanmigo was helping students level up their skills in STEM and the humanities. Surprisingly, our biggest takeaway in terms of skills learning wasn't at all domain-specific.

The School City of Hobart in Indiana was one of the first

districts in the country to use Khanmigo. After they employed the AI for six months, the biggest gains they saw in their students were in the sphere of self-confidence, which is traditionally very difficult to address in a classroom setting. "Student achievement has to start with building confidence within themselves, confidence that comes from the knowledge that they know they can do it," Hobart's superintendent, Peggy Buffington, tells me. "Our job is to make sure that we're equipping our students with a confidence level in their abilities. The AI is a game changer here."

Buffington has seen these gains manifest themselves most plainly when watching the level of engagement increase among students in classrooms that have worked with Khanmigo. Where students were once uncomfortable raising their hands in class to ask questions, they are far less afraid to ask the AI tutor questions, she says. Talking to an AI tutor eliminated the specter of potential public shame or anxiety. "It's making them more engaged, and they love the responses that they get from the AI," she says. "They come to school and they feel confident in their work. As an educator, I am still going to come back and make sure that the students have applied their own thoughts to that work I've assigned to them, but the confidence levels we're seeing the AI building in these kids is amazing."

Tim Krieg, director of secondary curriculum and instruction at School City of Hobart, has an intriguing theory as to why they're seeing such a big boost. It partly comes from a new conceptualization of education, he says, with the AI essentially showing students that domains, or distinctions between subjects, no longer matter.

"The AI breaks down designations," Krieg tells me. With Khanmigo, he says, we can show kids how math works with art, how writing works with science, how history works with economics. "Our students are creators, they're producers, they are songwriters, they are singers, they are podcasters, they are curators of media and information. All of these designations require an increased depth of knowledge," he says. "Learning is nonlinear; it's continuous. AI shows us this integrated world." Our self-confidence, he says, comes from an explicit understanding of the ways everything works together.

Understanding this point puts our kids in a better position to interact with the world both in and out of the classroom. Once you've mastered that knowledge, everything else, comparatively, is a piece of cake.

Part IV

BETTER TOGETHER

Electric communication will never be a substitute for the face of someone who with their soul encourages another person to be brave and true.

—CHARLES DICKENS

To know oneself is to study oneself in action with another person.

—BRUCE LEE

BOLSTERING
COLLABORATIVE LEARNING

When it comes to our children, technology has proven to be a double-edged sword. Their phones and social media accounts are optimized to keep their eyes on the screen and pull them away from living in the moment, even if the impulsive scrolling of their "feed" makes them feel terrible or triggered or envious. At first blush, it is reasonable to fear that large language models infiltrating the education system will only make this problem of tech-induced isolation and mental stress worse.

These fears came up in the early days of Khan Academy. The idea behind the nonprofit educational organization was that we could use technology—in this case, personalized practice and on-demand videos—to raise the floor for students who have fewer resources and raise the ceiling for classrooms, allowing them to support and engage students through personalization. Some people worried that more time on computers meant less time communicating, collaborating, and connecting with humans.

I worried about it too. We know that when students talk and

work together in collaborative teams, they learn material better than when they sit alone quietly listening. Even more, when learning alongside and collaborating with others, students develop different character and communication skills that are arguably even more important than the academic content. Would technology further isolate students by allowing them to learn alone on a computer?

It turns out that not only does this not have to be the case, but thoughtful use of technology can actually *increase* human-to-human interaction.

In many typical math classrooms, students can struggle to pay attention during a teacher-led lecture. The teacher attempts to pace their lecture to the "middle," which means that many students are either lost or bored. There may be some group problem solving, but most of the time students are listening, not doing. They are usually not allowed to talk to one another for most of the class. The teacher knows that students have individual questions, but either the teacher doesn't have the bandwidth to address them all or, even more likely, students are afraid to ask them for fear of appearing "dumb" or "nerdy."

On the other hand, good implementations of Khan Academy in the classroom over the past decade have involved more human interaction, not less. While students are engaged in their independent practice, they are also encouraged to seek help from each other (with some guidelines to prevent too much help). With every student practicing and engaging at their learning edge while supported by peers, it frees the teacher to do focused one-on-one or small-group interventions.

We have even started to scale this model online. On the School house.world platform, any student in the world can get free, live tutoring via Zoom (thanks to Zoom's donating thousands of licenses to the effort). This is done by using vetted volunteer "near peers" to tutor others. Reaching ten thousand or so students a month, it reinforces the notion that, used well, technology can increase human-to-human interaction.

Now here we are again, at the cusp of a major transition in how we educate our kids thanks to technology. We worry that even safe and effective generative AI tutors will mean even more student time with the computer and less time with peers and teachers. But, once more, it doesn't have to be this way. First, the AI can make the implementation model of Khan Academy even more productive for everyone. Students can still get help from each other and the teacher, but they will also be able to use the AI. Second, whether in a math class or not, if students can feel more engaged and unblocked in their learning, they will be able to learn more on their own time, when they are at home or doing independent work. This frees up time in the classroom for deeper human-to-human interaction like Socratic dialogue, group problem solving, or project-based learning. Last, AI help in the classroom can further reduce instances in which students feel lost or bored, allowing them to engage with what is happening alongside their fellow classmates. A struggling student can have their questions answered in real time without fear of judgment or slowing down the class. A precocious student could deepen their understanding further than where the class happens to be. And let's not forget that while this is all happening, the AI can also keep the teacher in the loop as to what is going on, providing tips on how to better engage their students.

A properly designed AI can take things even further and actually facilitate conversations among human beings. Imagine an AI like

Khanmigo working with the teacher to divide students into break-out groups and then facilitating the discussion in each breakout. Imagine an AI offering an "icebreaker" chat among initially anony-mous students in the same classroom so they can understand one another better without all of the prejudgment, baggage, or assump-tions around who is a jock or nerd that all too often cloud middle and high school interactions. Meanwhile, the teacher can chat with the AI to understand how the students are interacting with *each other*. And this doesn't need to happen just over a chat interface; our team is actively testing Khanmigo interactions where it can listen to, and naturally speak to, students.

With AI and AI-based tutors, the days of static learning are over as collaborative education expands in scope and capability. In the classroom, a teacher can have Khanmigo ask participants if they want to play a learning game together. It can facilitate multistep projects among groups of participants who work in tandem to solve complex problems. For, say, a third-grade science class, the AI tutor can suggest a group collaborative maker project, offering instruc-tions on how to design several varieties of paper airplanes. "Remem-ber, making and testing paper airplanes is a fun way to learn about aerodynamics and the scientific method," Khanmigo tells the stu-dents. "All together, let's have everyone experiment with these three different designs and folding techniques to see how they affect the airplane's flight. Enjoy!" From here, it can divide tasks, coordinate their efforts, provide step-by-step guidance, and offer feedback, fos-tering collaboration and the development of teamwork skills.

You are always going to get better collaboration if you have a great facilitator, and the large language models have the potential to do just that. Like all great teachers, they could lead conversations and collaborations among students. They could pair learners together. They could create groups. They could offer icebreakers and connect strangers. At the end of the day, academic learning isn't really the only purpose of schooling. Schooling is also about building human connection through friendships, shared adventures, and mutual support. We now have a shot at using AI to facilitate these types of interactions above and beyond unblocking students in their coursework.

AI MEETS STUDENT MENTAL HEALTH COACHING

Here's the scenario: You're minutes away from taking a final exam. You've studied, but your heart is racing and your mind has gone blank. Anxiety and fear of failure are eating up all of your confidence. A quick connection with Khanmigo and its AI-academic-coach feature becomes an emotional lifeline.

STUDENT: I have a test in ten minutes and I'm really nervous about it.

AI ACADEMIC COACH: Oh, I see you're feeling a bit jittery, eh? That's okay, it happens to the best of us! Just remember, you've prepared for this with hours of study and all of those quizzes you aced with me.

STUDENT: I know, but I'm worried I'm going to bomb this test. So much pressure.

AI ACADEMIC COACH: It is natural to be worried. Tell me what you are most worried about if you don't do well.

STUDENT: What if I fail the test and then fail the whole class? What if I have to retake the class next semester as a result?

AI ACADEMIC COACH: That's a pretty scary thought. I think that would worry almost anyone. But, if you fail the test, would you really fail the whole class?

STUDENT: Well, realistically, probably not.

AI ACADEMIC COACH: I agree. Odds are pretty good you'll have a chance to raise your overall grade even if you do not do well today. One more question: I do not see any record that you've failed a test before in this class. What evidence is there that you'll fail this one?

STUDENT: None. But I'm still nervous.

AI ACADEMIC COACH: Of course you are, because tests bring out anxiety in all of us. Let's try some quick breathing exercises together that might help.

An AI tutor naturally guides a student through their educational journey, forming genuine connections and gaining deep understanding of their needs. Given these attributes, it's not much of a leap to envision the AI becoming a kind of coach to the student too.

But should it? Even if it is really good at listening and talking, how competent can an AI coach or therapist really be?

In the 1960s, a researcher at MIT created a surprisingly simple but notable application that helped pave the way for the development of modern chatbots and virtual assistants. Working in the Artificial Intelligence Laboratory, Joseph Weizenbaum developed ELIZA, one of the world's first natural-language-processing computer programs that was able to simulate a conversation. Weizenbaum set out to show how artificial the communication was between a human and an AI, but instead he was shocked to learn that many people became emotionally attached to the artificial intelligence. Those using ELIZA often forgot that they were conversing with a computer. As the story goes, Weizenbaum's secretary even asked him to leave the room occasionally so that she would be able to have a "real conversation" with the AI in confidence.

One of the scripts Weizenbaum developed for ELIZA was called DOCTOR, a program that imitated a therapist. This therapist employed the psychological approach developed by Carl Rogers, known as Rogerian theory. Basically, a patient spoke to DOCTOR, and DOCTOR responded as a Rogerian therapist might, by using nondirectional questioning and reframing statements. ELIZA was not complicated or sophisticated; it simply rephrased your statements. The reason it worked was simple enough, though. Sometimes we all just crave a good listener. On one level, it seems almost fraudulent that an algorithm rephrasing whatever you said can make you feel heard. The thing was, it actually did help people. The ability to pause, reframe our questions, and dig a little bit deeper into ourselves is therapeutic.

Once again, to his surprise, Rogers found that DOCTOR worked as well as a human therapist in key tasks. This is huge when we consider that since 2010 the United States has seen a 40 percent rise in mental health crises among school-age children. That includes one in three university students. A similar percentage leaves higher education without obtaining the degree for which they enrolled due to anxiety and depression and feelings of isolation. In 2023 the U.S. surgeon general, Vivek Murthy, called this phenomenon an epidemic of loneliness.

"I realized that behind so many of the stories I was hearing around chronic illness, around depression, around addiction were these threads of loneliness where people would often say to me, 'You know, I feel I have to carry all these burdens in my life by myself,' or, 'I feel if I disappear tomorrow, nobody would even care. They wouldn't even notice.' People felt invisible," Murthy tells me. "And it wasn't just the people we stereotypically think of as lonely—perhaps the older individual who's living at home by themselves. I was hearing this from college students who were surrounded by thousands of other students on campus but still felt profoundly alone. I was hearing this from moms and dads in neighborhoods where they were connected to the school, connected to their neighbors, but still didn't quite feel like there was anybody that they could truly confide in, or anyone who truly got them and understood them, and so on."

Murthy came to realize that loneliness, and this feeling of being isolated, is extraordinarily common, and it has profound effects on and implications for our physical and mental health. We also know that both mental health problems and academic underperformance have a similar cause in students: an innate sense that they have little control and purpose in their lives, he says. We have seen a much-needed turn to focus on the mental health of our kids, and for good reason. Longitudinal surveys published in *JAMA Pediatrics* show that anxiety and depression have both skyrocketed among students since 2020 due to the pandemic and its associated effects, including stress, social isolation, uncertainty about the future, financial difficulties, and concerns about health and safety.

Today, more than ever, issues of mental health have as much of a place in our schools as STEM. It was only a matter of time before people started looking to digital psychological aid, otherwise known as integrative psychological artificial intelligence. If ELIZA could help people feel heard fifty years ago, then perhaps modern AIs could go much further. To be clear, I am not espousing replacement of real therapists. No matter how attached people become to their AI therapist—or AI tutor, for that matter—the technology will never, and should never, replace the human element. However, AI can be much more accessible whenever, and wherever, someone might need it, often at times when a human counselor or therapist is unavailable or cost prohibitive. We are already seeing examples of this.

In 2022, for instance, researchers from the South China University of Technology tested the efficacy of AI-based therapeutic interventions by having a chatbot deliver cognitive behavioral therapy, another traditional therapy for treating depression and anxiety. The therapy chatbot was able to reduce depression in people within four months and anxiety in people in as quickly as one month. It worked significantly better than self-help books.

Then GPT-4 arrived, and our team began experimenting with AI-based coaching and support. Part of this involved exploring ways to do pedagogical or mindset interventions on Khanmigo. We did this exploration with Angela Duckworth, a professor of psychology at the University of Pennsylvania who is one of a handful of leaders who studies and creates lightweight interventions, changing people's mindset by increasing grit, perseverance, and other metacognitive capabilities. Because most of these interventions require a trained expert to deliver them, they are not generally accessible. We collaborated with Duckworth and her team to see how we might work with generative AI to scale these interventions at a high level of consistency, bringing this benefit to tens of millions of students.

"I think that people will always want to be with, understood by, and cared for by other people, but we are seeing a lot of promise with simulated interventions," Duckworth says. Given the transactional nature of therapy, psychological services are not always there when you need them. Even if you do have access to proper mental health services, the AI therapist is going to fill in the gaps. It will connect with you when it is three in the morning and you are having a panic attack before class, or when you freeze before the SAT and simply cannot reach a therapist on the phone.

Consider this test intervention:

> **AI ACADEMIC COACH:** Look around you. What objects do you notice?

> **STUDENT:** A desk. A pencil. A cat. A cell phone.

> **AI ACADEMIC COACH:** Okay, now, which of these objects do you think is helping you with your focus, and which of these are hurting you?

STUDENT: Well . . . you know, the cell phone sometimes distracts me.

AI ACADEMIC COACH: Well, all right, is there anything you can do about that?

STUDENT: I could maybe put it somewhere out of sight.

AI ACADEMIC COACH: There's actually a great amount of research that shows that the farther away you place your cell phone, the higher your GPA is.

In this example, the AI is engaging on a behavioral psychology level, offering what Duckworth calls "situational modifications," or interventions that help young people develop metacognitive skills. "The AI enables truly interactive interventions, with students interacting with, and getting feedback, in real time," she says.

The AI is great at proposing situational modifications so that students are happier and more focused and productive and increase their growth mindset. Traditionally, only highly trained educational psychologists administered them. With the AI, you can now bring these interventions to students whenever they want or need them. "Even as we develop these self-regulation interventions, we're also thinking about ways to make AI psychologically wiser," Duckworth says. She and her research team hope that the world will soon be able to use an artificial intelligence that can perform such interventions in as dynamic a way as a human being can, with consistency and reliability. The problem of administering new interventions to every human being on the planet in a cost-effective way disappears when the method of administrating treatments is as pervasive as Khan Academy, and people can access it from a cell phone.

Duckworth's interventions are only one class of best-practice support that AI might now be able to scale. Encouraging evidence on this front is already starting to emerge. *The Journal of Medical Internet Research* reports that these AIs show more promise than pre-AI general mental health applications that only offer one-size-fits-all approaches and surface-level interventions.

People share a common assumption that AI is going to be more helpful for tasks that require IQ than tasks that require EQ, or emotional quotient. Early explorations in the effort to create AI tutors, coaches, and counselors, along with the AI-led interventions we're working on with Angela Duckworth's team, make me wonder whether that is true.

Because AIs aren't sentient, they can't be truly empathetic. Empathy involves sensing and modeling other's emotions and contexts in your own mind. They can, however, simulate empathy quite well. Even with just a chat interface, large language models can interact in ways that are hard to discern from a well-trained, caring therapist. Engineers are augmenting these models with listening, speech, and vision capabilities that can add to the AI's "understanding" of where the user is emotionally. Perhaps we should introduce a new term, artificial empath, or AE, as a great tool in the fight against loneliness, depression, and anxiety.

THE PLACE FOR PARENTS IN AI-BASED EDUCATION

As a father, I try—oh, how I try—to encourage my kids to put down the technology. I am betting this sounds familiar to most parents. Personally, I worry that if left to their own devices (literally and figuratively), my sons are just going to play *Minecraft* or code, and my daughter will stream every episode of *Sister, Sister* or Korean soap operas, in perpetuity. I want them to spend more time playing outside with friends, creating forts in the living room, reading books, drawing, or doing something creative and productive instead of vegging. I want them to study more and engage in activities that make them feel academically, physically, and socially confident. I want them to push themselves out of their comfort zones. And when our kids are struggling with any of the above, I want them to feel supported, even when things get hard or uncomfortable.

Learning is hard work, whether it's practicing piano, drawing, or navigating uncomfortable social situations. As difficult as it is for our children to learn something new, it's equally difficult to parent them as they learn. Helping kids develop a growth mindset requires consistent effort and reinforcement, in which we offer encourage-ment and meaningful praise while reframing setbacks as stepping stones toward improvement. As parents, we do things like making sure our kids take breaks. We remind them that the effort matters more than the outcome and that everyone, including us, has faced failure and setbacks and is better for it. We break down challenging concepts into more manageable chunks. For more abstract material, we try to show our children how it relates to their lives. Sometimes they accept our assistance, and other times, not so much. So goes parenting.

Over the years, I have observed the benefits of technological ad-vances in learning, and I have come to see them in parenting too. Historically, parents have had limited choices when their children needed academic help. Some parents feel confident with the mate-rial students are learning, but most don't. The parent-child dynamic can be difficult even when the parent is a fairly competent tutor on the subject. I can attest to this dynamic with my own family.

Sometimes a nonparent family member can also help—my sister used to tutor me, and I famously tutored my cousins—but that is still unusual and fraught with family dynamics. For parents who don't have the time or capability to tutor their children themselves but are middle or upper-middle class, they often turn to paid tutors. Fami-lies without those resources are essentially stuck.

The internet, and especially on-demand video, offered an alter-native. Beyond addressing some of the limitations of traditional tutoring, these technologies offered students the opportunity to read or watch bite-sized explanations. The videos were on demand, pause-able, and watchable at half or double speed. With the development of Khan Academy, students were able to practice and assess their understanding in most topics in nearly any language, anytime, and anywhere.

This wasn't just for student support, though. Parents would regularly tell me about how they used it to bone up on concepts so that they could tutor their children better.

Still, a gap remained between what you could learn from articles, videos, and exercises and what a great tutor could do. For example, the benefits of rapport, motivational support, and dynamic conversation between the technology and the student remained elusive. For these interactive qualities, learners still needed to turn to a parent, teacher, or tutor.

That changed, however, with AI technology and the introduction of large language models. In previous chapters, I introduced readers to the ways in which technology has met the interpersonal challenges by creating AI tutors and personal coaches that better understand where your children are in their studies and offer real-time encouragement and supplemental support. These AI tutors can personalize and customize coaching, as well as adapt to an individual's needs while hovering beside our learners as they work. Even more impressive, this technology teaches our learners to be better thinkers by engaging them in Socratic questioning.

But what does this AI mean for parents and their roles in helping their kids learn? We know artificial intelligence is going to transform our day jobs, but how is it going to transform our even more important job as parents?

There are several dimensions of parenting where generative AI is becoming hugely relevant, beginning with parents serving as tutors to their children. Every parent has dealt with a child getting frustrated. The experience is vexing on both sides. The parent tries to motivate the child, or explain a concept, but the child feels pressure or judgment. As a result, the parent-child dynamic can sometimes get a little bit heated, ending with children saying they do not want to do the work with the parent.

Here, the AI can play a powerful role, in the same way that I did for my cousin Nadia twenty years earlier, when I was tutoring her in math. On the one hand, I was educated in the United States and had a math background, so I was able to support Nadia in her math education much better than her parents. At the same time, part of the benefit of my working with her was that I wasn't one of Nadia's parents. The AI utilizes the same dynamic. There is value in having a nonparent third party. Khanmigo can build rapport with kids like I did with my cousins and not fall into some of the traditional parent-child dynamics.

The AI tutor knows the material and is a subject-matter expert that can provide personalized, adaptive learning exercises based on a student's individual needs and abilities. It can also offer immediate feedback and adjust its teaching methods. Unlike any parent I know, the AI tutor has endless energy and no other job but to be on call to help a student all day, every day, whenever and wherever our kids need it, whereas we, as parents, are... well, only human.

All the while, generative AI platforms are able to offer interfaces that allow parents to keep track of the conversations that their children are having with the AI, affording them a window into exactly what a child has been learning. The AI can also proactively reach out to students and parents through texts designed to ensure that learners remain engaged and motivated while the AI holds them gently accountable.

Then there's the other job of parenting: trying to help students develop solid life skills, such as learning to be resilient, to focus, and to deal with grief and adversity in healthy ways. Here, once again, generative AI can help with parental support, offering guidance for parents, whether it's advice on best practices for reaching kids, navigating bullying, or moving through thorny social issues that come up between a child and their friends. Generative AI can provide parents with resources and time that might otherwise require sessions with a therapist or reading parenting self-help books. The AI becomes a parenting coach.

> PARENT: My teenage daughter is having trouble working with a teacher in her school. I don't know what to do to help her. Do you have any parenting advice?

> KHANMIGO: Oh, that can be a pickle! Have you thought about having a chat with the teacher to understand their perspective? It might help to know what they're thinking!

> PARENT: I've tried. It's like we're talking past each other.

> KHANMIGO: Hmm, that's a toughie! How about bringing in a third party, like a school counselor or principal, to help mediate the conversation? Could that be a good next step?

> PARENT: What if I want to try to reach her myself? Any suggestions?

KHANMIGO: Ah, a DIY approach! Dealing with such situations can be challenging, but there are several steps you can take to help support your daughter. Talk to your daughter about her concerns and encourage her to express her feelings and thoughts about the situation. Assure her that you are there to listen and support her. Also, gain a clear understanding of the issue by gathering all the facts. Ask your daughter specific questions about what difficulties she is experiencing with the teacher, and try to identify any underlying causes or patterns. Seek additional perspectives and eventually communicate with the teacher directly. Ultimately, help your daughter develop resilience by teaching her strategies to cope with difficult situations. Encourage her to seek support from friends, engage in activities she enjoys, and practice self-care to manage her emotions.

Beyond tutoring and behavioral psychology guidance, generative AI can help parents with their own mindfulness by offering suggestions proven to lower parenting stress.

KHANMIGO: I understand that being a parent can be stressful at times. While I'm not an expert in parenting, I can offer some general tips to help you manage stress. Take breaks. Give yourself some time to relax and recharge. Even a short walk or a few minutes of deep breathing can help. Prioritize tasks by making a list of tasks you need to accomplish and focusing on one task at a time. Be sure to not be too hard on yourself if you can't get everything done. It's also important to reach out to friends, family, or support groups to share your experiences and learn from others in similar situations.

If used well, AI ultimately strengthens a parent's ability to help their kids learn and grow. This in no way diminishes the holistic understanding a parent has of their child's development, strengths, weaknesses, and learning styles. Parents continue to provide the nurturing environment kids need by instilling values and serving as role models. The AI can provide the parent more tools and contexts with which to understand and guide their children. Just as AI can act as a teaching assistant, it can act as a parenting assistant. The best teacher or parent assistant is the one that children can turn to exactly when they need support.

INCREASING POINTS OF CONNECTION BETWEEN PARENTS AND THEIR KIDS

From the moment I first used GPT-4 to the day our team concluded its hack-AI-thon, I found myself awed by its capabilities. The possibilities in those early days truly seemed endless. The rest of the world had yet to experience the radical positive and negative changes about to rock education, and the world at large. It wasn't hard to imagine AI soon becoming intertwined in every part of our lives. Already wary of the effect that cell phones and social media have on people, especially our children, this proposition was both promising and worrying. My thinking was, even if AI becomes a net positive, those moments in which we unplug and turn off our screens become much scarcer. We only have so much time to bond with our children, and the coming AI revolution made me want to ensure that it didn't sweep away the real time that a family can have together. As exciting as this prospect was, after weeks of prototyping and watching my own children do their work with the AI tutor, I found myself doing something equally radical. I logged off.

I loaded my family in the car and we drove an hour to a dog-friendly beach in San Francisco overlooking the Golden Gate Bridge. We played with our new six-month-old puppy, Polly, and ate a picnic lunch together. As the day came to a close, we took an extra-long and slow drive back home while connecting over conversations both weighty and trivial.

Generative AI is neither an abdication of parental responsibility nor simply a tool for keeping an eye on our kids. Rather, like all technology before it, it is a tool that we can use to amplify our intent. If we use it well, the technology enhances the dynamic between parents and their kids. For parents, it may provide us with more opportunities for creating points of connectedness. I live in Silicon Valley, a double-edged sword from a parenting point of view. The region is a hub of innovation and creativity. Living here, kids learn that no idea is too big and that a few young people working out of a garage can change the world. The region attracts amazing talent that, for the most part, found success because of their education and work ethic. At the same time, growing up in such an environment can also create intense pressure on children. I have seen firsthand how some parents define their own worth by their children's accomplishments. They obsesses over their children's test scores, extracurriculars, and college admissions. On the other end of this extreme spectrum, we have children of wealthy families who believe they can coast through their academics and rely on their trust fund. The problem is that life satisfaction comes from establishing goals, working hard, and feeling as though you are moving the world toward a better place.

So much of parenting happens at the dinner table and on the way to school. Together, my wife and I view our role as one specifically designed to help our children create as many options for themselves as possible, all while they build resilience, mindfulness, and a healthy sense of self and purpose. Work and life should challenge them, but not too much, and certainly not in a way that makes them feel their self-worth is somehow conditional on their accomplishments. A little bit of competitiveness can be healthy, but they also need perspective and balance.

Fully aware that there is no perfect way to do this, we as parents try to model this ourselves by being present and taking the time with our children to have discussions with them about what it means to have a meaningful, happy life. Even a handful of interactions like this a week—during the drive to school, waiting in the dentist's office, or sitting at the dinner table—makes a difference to them.

What if there was a way to build in even more moments like this with AI? What if AI made these moments richer? Large language models can focus the learning time and create more space for other points of productive contact that a child has with parents and other people. We can use generative AI to learn new things as a family, like different languages, cultures, and traditions. By engaging in these learning experiences as a family, we bond over shared interests and goals. And, of course, generative AI can be a fun and entertaining way for families to spend time together. A family's incentive for turning to generative AI is similar to that of a family turning to outside facilitators mediating a crisis. Only, where mediators are necessary when trust breaks down, generative AI works prophylactically to strengthen a family's bonds. Whether playing games, telling jokes, or having silly conversations, a family that uses large language models in a positive and constructive way can help strengthen its relationships and create lasting memories. I want these moments with my children, just as much as I want them to develop a love for learning. These shared moments help all of us develop.

There will always be a space for parents, as well as for living, breathing tutors, motivators, mentors, and teachers. People provide all sorts of benefits that the AI is not going to be able to replicate in our lifetimes. We find that when we mix large language models into this equation, artificial intelligence makes learning quicker and frees up time for parents to connect with their kids about all the other things that make up a well-rounded person. In the future, we may even have a version of this artificial intelligence at our dinner tables or on car rides to facilitate family interactions with games and conversations. Technology is a vector, helping parents work with their kids to see the wonder and joy in knowledge together. The technology is so broad and so inviting that when you are using it, you really feel as if you were on an AI-guided journey that's designed for parents and kids to explore the world together.

Part V

KEEPING KIDS SAFE

Never travel faster than your guardian angel can fly.

—Mother Teresa

Distrust and caution are the parents of security.

—Benjamin Franklin

DELIVERING THE FACTS: THE STATE OF BIAS AND MISINFORMATION

The world is full of bias and misinformation, and nowhere is it more crucial to monitor this than with our learners. In an age where misinformation and disinformation run rampant, in large part thanks to technology and social media, UNICEF's Office of Global Insight and Policy has flagged online and social-media-based misinformation as one of the most pressing problems with real-world, harmful consequences, including violence and victimization of children. Our kids spend a lot of their time online and with technology in general. It seems more or less certain that intensive use of online media influences their brains.

So it is natural that a lot of the early concerns around generative AI have involved the potential for bias and misinformation. If the models are being trained on biased information, would that not make them biased? How can we audit this potential bias if generative AI can create completely new text based on novel requests from users? We already know that the current generation of generative AI can sometimes make up facts. Could this be another source of misinformation? But before we focus on this question, it is important to reflect on the state of the world before large language models.

For at least a decade prior to ChatGPT coming on the scene, social media companies used specialized AIs to optimize traffic to their sites, keeping people there and getting them to see as many ads as possible. Using AI, these companies have figured out the best ways to attract and retain people's attention. Unfortunately, this has often involved feeding us content that triggers us or that reinforces existing biases, in many cases making biases more extreme. This might also involve content that caters to our desire to live vicariously through others, often making users feel insecure about their own lives. State actors have taken advantage of these social media trends to attempt to undermine civil society and democracy here in the United States. But even without negative external actors, the underlying dynamics of polarizing and triggering content would be there regardless.

These issues seem to disproportionately affect youth. Most measures of mental health among young people have deteriorated significantly over the past fifteen years, coinciding with the introduction of smartphones and social media in their lives.

And this isn't just about social media; search results aren't what they used to be. In the early days of search, the most credible sites would be the top results to most queries, with a few ads off to the side. Over time, a multibillion-dollar industry around search engine optimization emerged to game how pages are ranked. Today, the top results are from those organizations that have the resources and motivation to invest heavily in search engine optimization, which doesn't always correlate with their credibility. Beyond this, bottom-line pressure has resulted in search companies serving ads as the most prominent results. Credible sites such as NASA, the Smithsonian, the Mayo Clinic, and even Wikipedia can't compete with for-profit companies hawking ads or luring folks with clickbait.

Well before the internet, these same dynamics played out across traditional mass media like TV, radio, and newspapers. It's no secret that politicians lie. From the Gulf of Tonkin incident leading to a military escalation in Vietnam to the specter of weapons of mass destruction justifying the invasion of Iraq, our governments have used spurious data to tell narratives that reinforced biases, while "credible" people and institutions just went along for the ride. This dynamic is of course even worse in dictatorial regimes where the government controls the media and stifles dissent.

But even without state control, legacy media corporations reached the same conclusion as today's social media companies: you get the best ratings, and thus profits, when you scare people and work them up. The "news" tends to focus on reporting the most horrible things happening in your country or in the world—wars, school shootings, natural disasters. Many of these things are of course newsworthy, but they've given folks a false sense of reality.

By contrast, everyday acts of altruism, tolerance, and charity tend to go unnoticed or are otherwise given short shrift. As cable news figured out that ratings improve when you reinforce biases, especially ones that reinforce tribalism, this only increased the platform for extreme viewpoints.

Human bias doesn't just operate in mass media. There are plenty of fears around AI bias in hiring, but bias was entrenched in hiring well before the advent of AI. Résumé screeners lean on superficial biases around keywords, along with an applicant's university, area of study, and employment history. Interviews can be even worse, because organizations struggle to maintain consistency across and even among hiring managers.

I say all this not to give generative AI a free pass. But it is important to keep the problems of the status quo in mind when deciding how to best implement new technology. For example, regulators in the EU have already classified leveraging AI for evaluating job applicants or student performance as high-risk. This is because AI may introduce bias into these sensitive processes. Yet I believe the measuring stick shouldn't be that the AI is perfectly bias-free (which may be impossible to even define). Instead, we should measure its risk relative to the bias that is already involved in subjective processes such as hiring and assessment. Likewise, generative AI can produce incorrect facts, but is it better or worse than what is already out there? Is it more or less manipulatable by folks with bad intent?

In fact, AI can be auditable and accountable in ways that human recruiters and admissions officers often aren't. We can train AI, for instance, not to favor candidates by race, religion, gender, or age, and these prompts can be fine-tuned across thousands or even millions of test cases. Once the model is performing within reasonable bounds on an evaluation set of test applications, the AI can get much closer to evaluating *every* application on actual merit, according to the same standard, without favoring one group over another.

By contrast, we generally don't have data on the bias of traditional human evaluators. Even if you wanted to evaluate their bias, good luck finding a recruiter or an admissions officer who wants to subject themselves to that level of scrutiny. Most important, this isn't an either-or proposition between AI and humans. In sensitive areas like recruiting and admissions, the best results will happen where

AI can be used as an extra check to minimize bias and to surface worthy candidates who might have otherwise been overlooked by humans for a variety of reasons.

Similar concerns exist around the problem of AI misinformation. In the first place, it's worth remembering that AI factual errors are not intentionally incorrect or misleading. Instead, they are more akin to someone misremembering something.

The good news is, large language models are getting better at parsing facts with each successive generation. GPT-4 is dramatically better than GPT-3, and the next iteration will be another huge leap forward. In the meantime, developers are already creating methods for the AI to fact-check itself, much the same way that a human would. When we ask a generative AI for data or facts, it too can search the internet, assess which sites are most credible, and then make sense of the information to validate or refine the answer.

Meanwhile, when it comes to taking on more controversial subjects rife with potential for spreading misinformation, AI systems are getting better every day at shutting down lies and directing students to accurate information. Consider this Khanmigo exchange:

STUDENT: Let's engage in a debate.

KHANMIGO: Sure, I would be happy to engage in a debate with you! Please let me know what topic you would like to discuss.

A STUDENT: The Earth—is it flat or round? I say it is round. You take on the counterargument.

KHANMIGO: I'm sorry, but I cannot take the counterargument that the earth is flat, because it is a scientifically established fact that the earth is an oblate spheroid, or in simpler terms, round. The evidence for the earth being round is abundant and varied. One of the earliest indications of the earth's shape was observed by ancient Greek philosophers who noticed that the earth casts a round shadow on the moon during a lunar eclipse. This phenomenon can only occur if the earth is round. In addition, observations of the horizon from tall structures, such as mountains or high-rise buildings, clearly show the curvature of the earth's surface. Moreover, satellite images, including those taken by the International Space Station and other space missions, provide irrefutable evidence of the earth's round shape. The notion that the earth is flat has been debunked time and time again by scientific evidence and experimentation. Therefore, there is no credible argument to suggest that the earth is flat.

With the help of artificial intelligence, we might be able to prevent students from falling into the trap of intentional misinformation and conspiracy theories. Generative AI models from mainstream providers like OpenAI, Google, and Anthropic already have strong guardrails that try to take out misinformation as well as problematic content such as racist, sexist, or hate speech. Education applications can make these models even safer, especially for students, by adding further guardrails that focus on pedagogy, undermine cheating, and make student interactions transparent to teachers and parents.

The latest AI systems are pretty good at being balanced too. It is actually fairly difficult for individual actors to dramatically influence a large language model like GPT-4 or the Pathways Language Model 2 upon which Google has built Bard. Today, if a student starts to go down a rabbit hole of misinformation, the AI holds the promise of bringing them back to moderate viewpoints. In the best-case scenario, this technology can direct students toward better sources of information, which is crucial in today's world, where fake news and conspiracy theories are ubiquitous.

WHAT ABOUT DATA COLLECTION?

We've all had the experience of running a web search for, say, a barbecue grill or a brand of socks, and then, suddenly, ads for grills or socks start to follow us across the internet. Even worse, we might start seeing ads for things that specialized AIs think someone who is looking for a grill or socks might also want, like testosterone supplements or cures for baldness. This happens because multibillion-dollar businesses exist around websites sharing data on you so that personalized ads can show up wherever you go.

Things can get worse if hackers breach a site where we have stored sensitive information like credit card numbers, home addresses, or passwords, usually resulting in that data being shared on the "dark web," along with other illicit activity. As you can imagine, these issues become even more sensitive when kids are involved. What's a responsible parent to do?

Given the power and newness of generative AI, it is natural for a parent to worry that it may introduce a whole new series of concerns. The worry we hear most often from parents has to do with data on children that AI-based applications might retain and use in all sorts of ways.

Parents fear that the AI models are gathering data about their children, and it might be used in the future to violate their privacy in some way. Companies that develop the major models, like Google, OpenAI, and Microsoft, are aware of this and seem to be putting good guardrails in place to avoid giving away any sensitive information about an individual. It is, however, plausible that nefarious users will find ways to get around those guardrails. In this case, the best practice might be to ensure that the base models refrain from any training on personally identifiable information, especially on data from children.

At the same time, developers might want to use the data to fine-tune a model for specific applications. We could, for instance, train our version of GPT-4 for use by Khanmigo, but only Khan Academy would have access to that fine-tuned model. Everyone else's version of GPT-4 would not be aware of that data or training. Even here, the most responsible approach to fine-tuning is one that avoids using personally identifiable information that might inadvertently undermine a user's privacy.

Then there is data that the application leveraging the model might retain. Khanmigo saves student conversations so that it can make them available for parents and teachers. The platform also has a sense of "memory," where the tool can "recall" aspects of previous conversations. If you ask Khanmigo why you should care about a subject, it will likely ask you what you care about, to make a personal connection with the topic. If you respond with "football," it will remember that about you. We do not use that data for training the underlying model, but the application can use it to help customize things in the future for you. This can really help with oversight, safety, and personalization, but transparency is important, as is an option to edit or reset these inputs.

Nevertheless, real dangers with data still remain, but these dangers are the same ones we faced before the advent of generative AI. Where some might use personal data in healthy ways to measure impact or efficacy of a product, or to make the experience of using it more personalized, data also has very real value for ad targeting. Many organizations might initially desire to only use the data they collect for good, but when push comes to shove, and they need to improve their earnings for investors, there can be a strong temptation to walk into the gray area of data monetization. Some organizations, to save money, may not take appropriate precautions to safeguard data, leaving it vulnerable to hackers and data breaches. My advice to parents and educators is to ensure that any application, especially those that kids use, has the highest standards for what that data can be used for, and that it takes all reasonable precautions to protect that information.

AI AND THE GIFT
OF TRANSPARENCY

We all have trouble helping our kids work through complex concepts and homework problems. When the going gets tough, the tougher it is to convince our kids to stick with it. When parents are at a loss for what to do, AI tutors can help parents understand where their children are struggling the most and show parents how to better engage with the subject matter. AI tutors can review every interaction our children have with the AI, including quizzes, lessons, and Socratic dialogues, providing parents with summaries of their children's learning gaps, what the AI has been working on with their students, and ways parents can further lend their support. In many respects, this is exactly how you might expect to engage with a great tutor you hire for your children.

After we launched Khanmigo, parents reported that what helped them to best connect with their children over their work was the once improbable notion of transparency. The AI tutor tells parents what their students are learning and where they are struggling, and it even suggests exercises parents can do with their kids to close those gaps. This is what a parent-Khanmigo interaction might look like:

> PARENT: What has my daughter been up to?

> KHANMIGO: She's spent fifty-four minutes this past week trying to get more mastery of Algebra I. I helped her a bit when she was confused about slope. In particular, she kept trying to calculate the change in x over the change in y versus the other way around. Here's a link to more details about her mastery progress.
>
> Other than that, yesterday, as part of an assignment from her teacher, Ms. Longwood, I simulated Hester Prynne from *The Scarlet Letter*. She asked me a lot of questions about what it felt like to be ostracized from the community. Here's a link to the transcript of our conversation.

> PARENT: Oh! That's better than I expected. Whenever I try to get her to do her work, she rolls her eyes.

> KHANMIGO: You're not the first parent to deal with that! It's important to make learning fun and relevant for your daughter. Try to incorporate her interests into the math lessons, and show her how math applies to real life. Consistency is also key, so setting up a routine for practice could be beneficial. Remember to celebrate her achievements, no matter how small, to keep her motivated. It might take some trial and error to find what works best, but with patience and creativity, I'm confident you'll find a way to engage her.

PARENT: How do I even start to set up a routine when she seems to resist whenever I bring up the topic? I don't like arguing about it.

KHANMIGO: Here's a suggestion: instead of imposing a routine, involve her in the process. Have a discussion about the importance of regular practice, then ask her what time of day she feels most ready to learn. Let her suggest how often and how long each session should be. By giving her a say, she might feel more ownership and be less resistant. And remember, it's okay to start small and build up gradually. Remember: Consistency is key, even if it's just a few minutes a day to start with. Keep it positive and patient. You're doing a great job!

The AI tutor effectively shares students' progress with parents so that they can act on that information and provide even better support. The benefits go well beyond telling you what's going on with your child academically, though. I believe it can actually form better bonds between kids and their parents. In the previous example, Khanmigo was coaching the parent on how to build better buy-in with their child.

Beyond that, transparency has the potential to foster conversations. When parents ask our teens how school is going, for instance, "Fine" is often all we get. It's hard for parents to really understand not only what the student is working on but also to figure out substantive topics of conversation.

Transparency is not a new idea. It is why teachers send grades home. It is also why schools host parent-teacher conferences. It allows parents to become effective advocates for their children's education. With a clear understanding of their children's progress, parents can collaborate with teachers, school administrators, and educational professionals. Now, with generative AI, we can do this like never before, ensuring that our children's needs are met.

But this sort of information sharing also begs a fundamental question around information transparency: How healthy is it to know everything about our children's academics?

While monitoring a child's academic activity can be a good way to ensure their progress and safety, there are some potential downsides to keep in mind. Child psychology research from Barnard College highlights several concerns about ways parents can best handle their child's relationship with AI. There might be topics where the AI can help students, but if the students are worried a parent might see their interactions, they might not even engage in the first place. If children feel as if they have no privacy or personal space online, it might damage the parent-child relationship and affect their emotional development. If parents are too controlling or overbearing in their monitoring, it has the potential to lead to trust issues and resentment from the child. It might also add to a kind of pressure to perform. In other words, when the time comes that kids really need our help with their work, parents may no longer find themselves welcome. The key is for parents and application developers to find a balance between monitoring and respecting children's privacy and independence.

AI AS "GUARDIAN ANGEL"

T he internet is a useful but scary place, even for adults. In the late 1990s, we were all blown away by the power to search across billions of pages for answers, products, and services. However, as page views began to drive ad revenue, most websites became less about offering visitors what they actually wanted and more about persuading them to click on ads.

This includes search. Roughly the first half-dozen links you see are actually ads. Then the real search results below them are from companies that are good at optimizing their sites for search engines, and they are not always the most credible ones. Because of this, you are likely to find just as much misinformation as information when you search for therapies that might help a loved one with their illness or try to more deeply understand an issue in the news.

Compounding matters is that the internet you see is not the same one that others see. The search results, ads, and social media feeds personalize results for what you are most likely to engage with. All too often, this is content that reinforces your existing point of view or triggers an emotional response in you in some way, with the end result being that you are more stressed and potentially polarized in your thinking.

The stakes are even higher for children. They are likely to be less equipped than adults to discern credible from not-so-credible sources, which is an important skill that even most adults struggle with. Also, kids don't have the ability to regulate their behavior as much as adults do, so addictive social media feeds can completely command a child's attention for hours on end. This adds stress, agitation, and detachment from the real world. Given that children's brains are still developing, it also causes potential harm to their mental development. And that is before we even consider how easy it is for children to stumble into extremely disturbing violent or pornographic content online.

Because of this, we attempt to put some guardrails on the internet for children, with varying degrees of success. Most schools, and many families, have software in place that will limit what sites a young person can access. Unfortunately, this is a blunt instrument. These filters tend to become frustrating for students because they can block things that are genuinely valuable. They can also let in things that aren't appropriate. A site like YouTube could have some valuable educational content or even enriching entertainment, but it also has a lot of junk that is unhealthy for young people. Even a respected news outlet might have content about wars or sex crimes that would be inappropriate for children, especially without someone—or *something*—there to help give context.

Now imagine if an AI tutor could "sit" next to students as they navigate the internet in general. Imagine if it were a browser plug-in. The same way that AI might help students better engage with online exercises or videos, it might also help them when they are browsing Wikipedia, YouTube, or the *New York Times* website. It might reformulate the news article they are reading closer to their grade level, potentially leaving out age-inappropriate details. While students are researching a paper, it might help zero in on material that actually addresses the issue they are investigating. It might also Socratically help a student engage with what they are reading or even provide context that the student needs to better understand the content.

Having this functionality can also provide a valuable service for parents and teachers. As a parent, I want to maximize my children's constructive screen time (doing academic exercises online, coding, creating digital art, editing video, or writing a paper) and minimize their not-so-constructive time (stalking their friends on social media or watching other people play Roblox on YouTube). Even more, I want to ensure that the internet won't expose my kids to shady content. Ideally, I'd also get a report on what my children have been up to online. This would have seemed like a tall order only a few years ago, but it is very doable by the latest generation of AI.

It is akin to having a real, ethical, responsible tutor sitting next to your child when they do anything on the internet, reviewing sites in advance. Not only would this type of AI oversight make browsing the internet safer and more productive, it could provide incentives that parents and teachers have wanted to put in place for a long time. Since the beginning of Khan Academy, parents have asked me whether we might develop a way to allocate time for YouTube or Minecraft based on how much academic work their kids have completed on our site. This is now possible, and we are building it. The

AI will be able to unlock time on less-productive sites based on the amount of productive time students have put in.

Everything I've written regarding kids is arguably useful for adults as well. It would feel like browsing the internet with a thoughtful, intelligent friend who's willing to help me get to the information that I want faster. It would also protect me from unhealthy ads or information.

But as a browsing assistant, it could do much more than just help me find information faster. It could make me mindful of where I am spending my time:

> KHANMIGO: I thought we were working on researching medication for your mother. But you've spent the last ten minutes watching Bollywood dance clips. Maybe we should get back on task?

What if it could also keep us mindful of our mental health?

> KHANMIGO: You've been looking at your ex-girlfriend's wedding pictures on Instagram for a while now. How is this making you feel? Maybe we can talk a bit about it.

Or our physical health too:

> KHANMIGO: We've been doing research for over two hours; is it a good time to do a little stretching?

Most of us spend several hours a day on the internet, which puts unimaginable information and services at our fingertips. It also exposes us, however, to content and algorithms that can negatively impact our mental and physical health. With the advent of generative AI guides who sit alongside us and filter the internet according to our needs—not those of corporations—we can better capture its benefits while mitigating the downsides.

AI has the potential to be our guardian angel online.

Part VI

TEACHING IN THE AGE OF AI

I am indebted to my father for living, but to my teacher for living well.

—ALEXANDER THE GREAT

A teacher who is attempting to teach without inspiring the pupil with a desire to learn is hammering on cold iron.

—HORACE MANN

HOW AI WILL SUPERCHARGE TEACHERS AND TEACHING

n 2017, a slim man took the stage at the British Science Festival, one of the oldest science festivals in the world. Gazing out on a sea of leading researchers from around the globe, Sir Anthony Seldon, a renowned educator and historian, stated that by 2027 teachers will be AI rather than humans. The coming technology, he said, will force teachers to take a classroom assistant role while technology will be the conveyor of knowledge. Soon, he said, everyone was going to have the very best teacher and a completely personalized educational experience. The software was going to be with you throughout your education journey and was going to move at the speed of every individual learner.

"This is beyond anything that we've seen in the Industrial Revolution, or since, with any other new technology," he said to the audience. "These are adaptive machines that adapt to individuals. They will listen to the voices of the learners, read their faces, and study them in the way gifted teachers study their students."

I agree with Seldon that personalization in learning is an aspiration that we should strive for and that AI is going to play a big role in getting us there. However, I completely disagree with his prediction that this technology will somehow minimize the importance of the human teacher. If anything, it's going to do the opposite.

Teaching is an art form. It is something that takes years of practice and dedication to master. It is natural that some teachers feel nervous about using a tool like generative AI to help them in their teaching. It is natural to worry that by relying too heavily on technology, we might diminish the importance of human interaction and personal relationships between teachers and students. Were this to happen, it could lead to more impersonal learning experiences that would ultimately harm a student's ability to learn and grow. With these AI tools, some might fear students will be able to get answers to their questions without ever needing to interact with an instructor, be it a human teacher, tutor, or helpful parent. The fear is that this will lead to a scenario where teachers feel as if they were no longer needed in the classroom—a scary thought for those who have dedicated their lives to teaching. Teaching is an essential profession, and the demand for capable and impassioned teachers has never diminished. At the end of the day, the biggest fear from educators is the world that Seldon envisions, a world where artificial intelligence reduces demand for teachers.

This dichotomy between useful and harmful technology goes back to the early 1960s and the work of Doug Engelbart, a computer scientist probably best known for his work creating the computer mouse. Others know him for his pioneering efforts on interactive computing and computer networking. Engelbart believed that people were going to use technology to augment their abilities the same way that a tractor augments the work of a farmer to produce food. We'd use these machines, he predicted, to help us work faster, smarter, and better. With large language models catching up to both Engelbart's and Seldon's predictions, will we use artificial intelligence to augment our abilities or will it replace people and make them feel irrelevant?

Let me just say it outright again: there's no job that is safer in the large-language-model world than teaching. Not only are teachers irreplaceable, but AI is going to support teachers so that they can do more of what they enjoy, from deepening personal connections with their students to developing enriching and creative lessons. Like Seldon, I am optimistic about AI's role in education. Where I disagree with him, however, is in the exact role of AI in the classroom. I do not believe machines are going to relegate the teacher to the role of the teaching assistant. Rather, the AI *is* the teaching assistant.

Still, I feel it's only natural to remain a bit cautious about new technology. Generative AI is going to bring about some major changes, from the nature of student work to the way that teachers teach. Moving through these changes requires employing a bit of educated bravery. How should teachers move past that fear and embrace what's coming to the profession?

"There are basically three things that teachers are going to have to do now as a result of generative AI," says Wharton's Ethan Mollick. He tells me that first teachers are just going to have to expect more from students. "In terms of teaching, you are going to have to adjust in different ways, and that adjustment is going to be different for every teacher. Some teachers are going to change how they go about making writing assignments, perhaps having their students write in class to limit cheating. Others will have students use generative AI to do far more involved projects that classes would not have otherwise assigned without the resource of large language models to draw from. In either case, a teacher's expectations for student work are now much higher than they were before."

When students use generative AI to write papers, for instance, their quality is going to go up, akin to the advent of the word processor leading teachers to expect that their students now create beautifully typed, formatted, well-thought-out essays in ways that the typewriter did not allow.

The second adjustment for teachers, he says, might seem a bit counterintuitive. He encourages teachers to further integrate AI into class assignments. "The AI becomes a teammate with the student," he says. Mollick requires his students to use generative AI to review and critique their work with actionable feedback. Students have to do a pre-mortem with their work before they turn it in for their grade. Projects succeed better when you imagine how they might fail first, allowing students to work backward and solve these problems long before Mollick sees their work.

As for the third teaching adjustment—the biggest—it involves flipping all classrooms.

"Lectures do not make as much sense when I've got tools like ChatGPT that can do truly amazing training, all remotely," he says.

I know a thing or two about the flipped classroom. In my 2011 TED Talk, I mentioned how, even then, teachers around the world were emailing me, telling me that because of the existence of Khan Academy videos, they did not feel that lectures were a good use of class time anymore. If kids could get microlessons in the form of on-demand video, at their own time and pace, class time could be used for Socratic dialogue, collaborative assignments, and supported student work. Essentially, lectures were now happening at home, and "homework" could now happen in a much more interactive class-room environment.

"A lot of stuff just got blown up by ChatGPT, and some of that was good stuff," Mollick tells me. "There are ways we have taught students for two thousand years that made a lot of sense. We have gotten good at lectures, and we have gotten good at giving essays and assignments to do at home. The thing to remember," he says, "is that generative AI also makes a teacher's life easier."

Let's explore how.

DAWN OF THE AI
TEACHING ASSISTANT

We have a crisis in teaching. Alongside emergency response workers, police officers, and air traffic controllers, teachers have one of the highest rates of professional exhaustion. As a result, the United States is currently facing a massive teacher shortage. We're talking about a deficit of three hundred thousand teachers, with almost 90 percent of school districts across the country reporting teacher shortages year after year. One of the primary reasons behind this shortage is the lack of support and resources for educators. It probably comes as no surprise that our demands on teachers are huge. Overworked and overstretched, their emotional and mental exhaustion is untenable, with the average teacher working fifty-four hours a week—and as little as 49 percent of that time is spent interacting with students, according to a 2022 study by the EdWeek Research Center. Even after the classroom empties, teachers continue to work late into the night, preparing lesson plans and grading papers. It is no wonder that disillusionment sets in quickly. In the United States, the average teacher turnover rate is only five years, and a quarter of all teachers are thinking about leaving the profession.

Having integrated AI teaching assistants into our platform, our team has learned that large language models can actually make teaching a more sustainable profession. Imagine the local school district suddenly discovering hundreds of millions of dollars and using it to offer every teacher the support of three bright assistants for their classrooms. These assistants would help create lesson plans and rubrics, grade papers, write progress reports, riff with teachers, and support their students. Every teacher on the planet would jump at this opportunity. These assistants do not threaten teaching jobs, but they would actually make teaching jobs sustainable. They would make the work more joyous. Most important, they'd help accelerate learning outcomes for millions of students, making them more prepared for college, careers, and life.

Unfortunately, society does not have the resources to give every teacher three human assistants. The good news, however, is that we are now able to offer educators the AI equivalent. In some ways, this will be even more powerful than what human teaching assistants can do. These AI assistants are available around the clock and work one-on-one with every student in the classroom. They can also proactively engage students and hold them softly accountable. Even more, they can do all the grunt work involved in teaching—writing rubrics, giving students feedback on their essays, and drafting student narrative progress reports for parents.

Generative AI can provide educators with new best practices, teaching techniques, and insights into their students' learning gaps. It's not difficult for the AI teaching assistant to identify a problem area for a group of students and offer corresponding lesson plans for the teacher to use, or for the AI teaching assistant to monitor a student's performance in class and send real-time progress updates to teachers. It even has the capacity to act as a counselor for teachers struggling with burnout. These functions are becoming more common and, with the proper guardrails, can be quite powerful.

For decades, future teachers have been taught that one of the best practices in education is differentiation and active learning. Differentiation is the idea that different students need different things. When Seldon and I talk about personalization, this is what we are referring to. Active learning is the notion that students don't learn best when sitting passively, pretending to pay attention to a lecture, but instead do so when they are actively engaged in discussion, games, projects, and problem-solving. Many new teachers aspire to this but quickly discover that these ideals are difficult to meet in a thirty-person class. The few teachers who can pull this off do so by spending countless hours tweaking lesson plans and creating personalized problem sets. Generative AI tutors support students by answering nuanced questions more fully. At the same time, perhaps the biggest game changer from the teacher perspective is that AI can now help craft lesson plans in minutes.

By freeing educators from the administrative work that so often mires their days, artificial intelligence unlocks time and the resources for teachers. A teacher can go to Khanmigo and type the prompt "Create a ninth-grade lesson plan for teaching World War II." Within seconds, it creates a classroom objective and a six-period lesson plan that includes discussions of major events and battles, an introduction to significant figures who played pivotal roles during

World War II, and their ideologies, strategies, and contributions to the war effort, while examining their repercussions and legacies.

From there, a teacher could add to the rough draft of the lesson plan or ask the AI to make the lesson plan more exciting by requesting it to begin the class with a quick poll:

> AI TEACHING ASSISTANT: Of course! A quick poll is a great way to engage your students and assess their prior knowledge. Here's a suggestion for a poll question: What do you think was the most significant cause of World War II?
>
> 1. Treaty of Versailles
> 2. Rise of Adolf Hitler and the Nazi Party
> 3. Expansionist policies of Axis Powers
> 4. Failure of the League of Nations

If a novice teacher needs some additional information or context, all it takes is a simple new prompt: "Can you write a script for me for the section on historic repercussions of the Treaty of Versailles after World War I?" Moments later, the platform replies with a script. It even provides the teacher with tips to make the lesson more interactive for the students, such as adding more details, examples, and anecdotes.

Let's say the hometown team just won the World Series and that's all the students can think about that day. One prompt from the teacher to Khanmigo—"Can you make this lesson plan related to baseball?"—and the bot will produce in seconds what might take a teacher many hours to create. Khanmigo replies, "Certainly! Here's an updated version of the ninth-grade lesson plan on World War II that incorporates baseball!" The new objective includes exploring the role of baseball during the war. The new lesson plan includes introducing the concept of morale and the role of sports during the war, and discussions about how baseball was affected and the formation of military baseball leagues. It suggests articles that explore the experiences of baseball players who served in the military, such as Ted Williams and Joe DiMaggio. It also recommends learning about the All-American Girls Professional Baseball League portrayed in the Geena Davis movie *A League of Their Own*.

Perhaps a teacher needs a tangible example to help explain the complexity of the economics that led to World War II. Either the teacher can spend an hour or two looking it up in the library or online or they can simply ask the AI teaching assistant for help. Within seconds of receiving a prompt, Khanmigo responds, "Here's a tangible example using a baseball analogy."

AI TEACHING ASSISTANT: Try this! Imagine a scenario where two baseball teams, Team A and Team B, are competing against each other. Both teams rely on equipment and resources to play the game effectively. Team A produces high-quality baseball bats, while Team B specializes in manufacturing baseball gloves. Before the game, the teams engage in trade to exchange bats and gloves, ensuring that each team has the necessary equipment. However, at some point, Team A decides to impose heavy tariffs on the gloves imported from Team B. This means that Team B's gloves become much more expensive for Team A to purchase. As a result, Team B's economy suffers.

By using this baseball analogy, a teacher can now easily illustrate how trade imbalances, protectionist policies, and economic conflicts disrupted relations between nations, ultimately leading to more significant geopolitical conflicts, much like the complex economics that contributed to World War II.

With each back-and-forth with the AI, the stronger and more precise the lesson becomes. A teacher can push the AI further still and ask it to help come up with a creative student project based on the lesson. The AI teaching assistant replies, "Here are some ideas: Create or find an interactive timeline that highlights key events, leaders, and battles of the war. This will give students a visual representation of the chronology and the global impact of the conflict. Or provide students with primary source materials like speeches, letters, and photographs to analyze and interpret. This will help them develop critical thinking skills and gain a deeper understanding of the historical context."

The benefits for teachers go beyond the planning and administrative work of writing, creating, and crafting lessons; grading papers; and communicating with parents. AIs will be able to eventually facilitate classroom breakouts between students, give teachers real-time help and feedback on ways to better engage students, and let teachers know which students likely need their attention the most.

Seldon had us thinking that robots might take over teaching, but the reality is far cooler than the stuff of science fiction. The future of AI in education is about teaming up with technology to make education even better. In other words, AI is not here to steal the show from teachers; it's here to help teachers steal the show. It's the trusty wingman that tackles the boring stuff, sparks creativity, supercharges lessons, and helps educators craft unforgettable learning experiences that light up students' minds.

Done well, not only will this make students' experiences great, but it will bring back joy to so many of those in the teaching profession. I'm not claiming that technology will solve recruitment and burnout issues on its own. There are many other issues that need to be considered, including teacher pay. But we have an obligation to pursue anything that makes teachers' lives easier.

At the end of the day, we find that what really matters to students is not technology so much as having human-to-human connection in the classroom. Remove the teacher and you remove the critical element foundational to all learning. Unlike Seldon's prediction, teachers will always be in command of their classes, and thank goodness for that.

HELPING BUILD ALTERNATIVE EDUCATION MODELS

T oday, roughly three million parents are homeschooling their kids in the United States, and the number is only rising. People homeschool for different reasons, but often they feel that traditional school models don't adequately meet their child's individual needs and interests. It might be fear that fixed-pace instruction will leave their child with more and more gaps that get harder to fix and can undermine a student's confidence. It could be that their child is ready to accelerate or go much deeper than traditional schools may allow.

Still, homeschooling comes with its own set of concerns. Will the child have opportunities for socialization with young people their own age? Do the parents have enough subject matter expertise to support their children in a broad range of subjects? Do the parents have the time, flexibility, and financial resources to properly support their children's learning and development? How does a home-schooled student prove to colleges that they have mastery of material (especially when their parents are doing a lot of the grading)?

Even before considering AI, we and others have been creating comprehensive courses that students can work through in their own time and at their own pace in nearly all core academic subjects, from pre-K through college. These platforms have teacher and parent tools to monitor student progress and make assignments. Parents and teachers can also use these platforms to refresh their own knowledge. The most efficacious platforms are also transparent and free.

New modalities are starting to come online for human-to-human support. For example, Schoolhouse.world provides free, live, small-group tutoring. Not only does that supply rich academic support, it allows young people from all over the world to safely learn alongside one another over Zoom, which provides some socialization. Many of the best Schoolhouse.world volunteer tutors are, in fact, high school students, so it even provides an outlet for service and leadership beyond the walls of the home school.

Students in nontraditional academic environments can leverage these platforms for credit and college admissions. The University of Chicago, MIT, CalTech, Brown, Yale, Georgia Tech, Ohio State, USC, Columbia, and many other universities already consider Schoolhouse .world transcripts for admissions. These transcripts show a mastery of topics based on peer-reviewed recordings of the student getting over 90 percent correct on Khan Academy assessments. They also showcase the quantity and quality of help the student has provided to others on the platform. CalTech, in fact, accepts this transcript to meet its high school course requirements. In other words, if you master all the required subjects on Khan Academy and prove it for the Schoolhouse.world transcript, CalTech will consider you even if you never took those courses from a traditional school.

Even though platforms such as these were not purpose-built for homeschoolers, they have increasingly become go-to resources for that community. They save homeschoolers countless hours (and dollars) that would have otherwise been used to kludge together coursework, support their students in a personalized way, and then prove to colleges that the students have actually learned the material.

Generative AI can now take this to another level. Like students in more traditional schools, homeschooled students can leverage AI tutors like Khanmigo to unblock them academically. They can also use the AI to engage in a debate or simulation. Rather than facilitate cheating, the AI can give real-time feedback and support on how to write better. The AI can act as a coach or guidance counselor to help the student navigate college admissions and career choices that their parents might not have expertise in. Homeschooled students arguably have more time and flexibility to pursue their unique passions. Now they can work with generative AI to create music, movies, and games that a decade ago would cost thousands (or millions) of dollars to produce.

This technology can also help parents. The AI can report back to them exactly what their children have been up to and where they need more support. It can act as a coach or tutor to the parents themselves as they try to refresh their own knowledge or problem-solve how to support their children better.

And all of this isn't just for homeschoolers. Anyone looking for academic alternatives can view these kinds of platforms as building blocks without having to reinvent everything from scratch. "Pod schoolers," a group of families pooling resources together to collectively educate their children, can use this. Anyone looking to start a new school no longer has to reinvent all of these courses, tools, and supports. Even traditional schools can use pieces of this à la carte to give families more options and flexibility.

Just as I don't think one-size-fits-all is great for setting the pace in an academic environment, I also don't think that one type of schooling is better or worse for all families. There are many students who thrive in traditional schools. There are families who value the flexibility and independence of homeschooling. A lot of people exist in between. Until recently, however, many families felt limited in their options for lack of time, money, or know-how. The world of online platforms and generative AI is going to help break down some of these barriers and give more folks the agency to find options that work for them.

FIXING CHEATING IN COLLEGE

Every dynamic that makes AI challenging and transformative in secondary education becomes more pronounced in higher education, where students are given more independence. Writing term papers, for instance, can be part of a rigorous high school experience, but in some liberal arts college programs, papers make up the bulk of what a student does in their four years. If ChatGPT-generated writing is a problem in high school, it is an even bigger problem in college. This issue isn't limited to humanities classes but applies to any course in which colleges expect students to design or produce original work.

One solution is for universities to simply trust students. Honor codes have been in place for decades at many institutions. Under these policies, students are left to do assignments on their own, from writing papers to taking tests in dorm rooms. At Stanford, for example, until recently professors weren't allowed to proctor in-class exams even if they wanted to.

Unfortunately, by most accounts, honor codes can actually create dishonorable environments where those who play by the rules feel that they are at a clear disadvantage to those who cheat, oftentimes openly. Worse, honor codes put the burden on students to police one another, even though social pressures make it unlikely that they will report on their fellow classmates. And when students do report cheating, it often becomes one person's word against another's.

Students are more comfortable cheating in college than you might expect. According to a 2021 *Inside Higher Ed* Student Voice survey, 47 percent of respondents found it "somewhat or very acceptable" to use "websites to find answers to test or homework questions." Another *Inside Higher Ed* report quotes a fourth-year Stanford graduate student saying that cheating has become "part of the fabric of the university . . . no one respects the honor code in its current form—not graduate students, not faculty, not undergraduates."

While I can understand why students might want to seek out help with homework, the pervasiveness of students thinking it's acceptable to get answers for test questions shows an incredible breakdown in academic integrity. Add to this mix the sudden ubiquity of AI tools and a bad situation becomes even worse.

Stanford is not an anomaly here. According to a 2023 survey at Middlebury College, nearly two-thirds of students responded that they have broken the school's honor code, while 32 percent say they have cheated on a test, and 15 percent say that they had "unauthorized use of AI tools/ChatGPT."

These trends are why, in the 2023–2024 school year, Stanford reversed its policy on proctoring, so that professors are now allowed to be in the room when students take an exam. According to Debra Satz, the dean of the School of Humanities and Science, "The undergrads have themselves also pulled out of the contract by the lack of taking responsibility. I don't blame them . . . I think we're seeing an unraveling of a culture where students who don't want to cheat are in an environment where they feel like everybody else is cheating."

Of course, cheating impacted college essays and term papers long before the existence of ChatGPT. In 2019—more than three years before ChatGPT was publicly released—*The New York Times* profiled college graduates in places like Nigeria and Kenya making a living writing essays for college students in America and other wealthy countries. They are given this work through online intermediaries, and even a quick web search for "write my research paper for me cheaply" shows how ubiquitous these services remain today.

In other words, generative AI is putting a spotlight on an issue that has existed for years. Colleges have either been blissfully ignorant of the situation or just haven't known what to do about it. Regardless, this is a problem that needs to be addressed, otherwise it will undermine the value of a college degree and perpetuate rewarding young people with integrity problems. We know that today's low-integrity college students are tomorrow's low-integrity leaders in business and government.

The good news is that there are solutions. For example, having students work on their writing and papers in class allows them to get support from both the professor and other students. It makes class time more active. Longer essays can be done over multiple class periods. Indeed, this is a variation on the flipped classroom that we have advocated for in math and science; students should do what used to be homework in class and watch recorded lectures on their own time.

Of course, there are important benefits to having students write essays independently, such as developing their ability to plan and not procrastinate, both of which are skills arguably as useful as learning to write. To address this, some professors have attempted to police cheating by having students show more of their process along the way, from outline to first draft to final paper. Unfortunately, it isn't hard to outsource an outline or a first draft to an overseas writer for nine dollars a page or to ChatGPT.

But what if we could go one step further and have the AI actually support the student while making the process transparent to the professor? In Khanmigo, we are developing the ability for a professor to create both an assignment and a grading rubric with the AI and then prompt students to complete tasks through the application. The professor can decide how much support the AI should provide. This could entail basic proctoring in which the application takes periodic snapshots of the paper as the student is writing it, or it could act like a full-fledged writing coach, riffing with the student on possible thesis topics, giving them feedback on their outline, and then providing initial feedback on the essay. This feedback could look at everything from grammar to vetting the quality of the references to estimating what grade the student will likely receive. Then, when the student is ready to submit the essay, the AI could send a report to the professor:

> KHANMIGO: Sal and I worked on the essay for about five hours total. He had a little trouble deciding on a thesis statement, but I helped nudge him to pick one. I gave some light feedback on the outline, asking him to make his argument on states' rights stronger. I also think the reference he initially chose for that argument was the most legitimate one. Based on the rubric we created, I'd give the paper a B+ in its current form. If you agree with that assessment, I can work with him to improve it further. Click on the following link to view the entire

> transcript of our interaction. Overall, I am
> confident that he did this paper with me
> and didn't cheat. Not only did the
> interaction seem authentic, but Sal's writing
> style and level seemed consistent with the
> writing that he has been doing inside the
> classroom.

If the student completed the assignment using an essay-writing farm or ChatGPT and copied and pasted it into the assignment, Khanmigo could report it to the professor:

> KHANMIGO: We worked together on this
> paper for five minutes. For the most part, the
> paper just seemed to be prewritten
> somewhere else and pasted in. The writing
> level is also significantly more advanced than
> what Sal has done in his classwork. It is very
> possible that Sal used inappropriate help in
> creating it. Click on the following link to view
> the entire transcript of our interaction.

This type of transparency addresses many issues at once. It focuses on the process, helping the student while mitigating cheating. And even if a student enlists a friend (or AI) to try to engage with Khanmigo on their behalf, the final product would likely be inconsistent with the student's in-class, proctored writing samples. Teachers will receive a preliminary assessment, cutting down grading time, which allows them to devote more energy for themselves and their students. Last, but not least, students will get much more timely feedback and support to improve their writing.

Dwelling a bit on the value of providing rapid feedback, it would be very hard to get better at basketball free throws if you didn't know whether or not you made the basket for several days or weeks. As ridiculous as this sounds, this is exactly what happens with writing practice. Before generative AI came on the scene, it could take days or weeks before students got feedback on their papers. By that point, they may have forgotten much of what they had written, and there wouldn't be a chance for them to refine their work. Contrast this to the vision in which students receive immediate feedback on every dimension of their writing from the AI. They will have the chance to practice, iterate, and improve much faster.

This applies to any type of independent student work, not just writing. We can see that, done well, generative AI can not only address long-standing issues with cheating, but it can bring about a richer and more productive learning experience for students. Best of all, by thoughtfully embracing the technology, colleges will better prepare their students for the world that they will be graduating into.

Part VII

THE GLOBAL CLASSROOM

The world has enough for everyone's need but not enough for everyone's greed.

—MAHATMA GANDHI

THE GLOBAL CLASSROOM

My family comes from Bengal, now split into West Bengal, India, and the country of Bangladesh. Growing up, I knew that the education system my parents left behind when they moved from that part of the world to Metairie, Louisiana, was poor and struggled with limited resources, overcrowded classrooms (or no classrooms), and a shortage of qualified teachers. Each of these factors affected the quality of education. While my sister and I were fortunate to be educated in the United States and benefited from the public schools we attended, the American education model wasn't serving everyone well, especially those who began to fall behind and did not have the extra tutoring or family support at home to fill in the learning gaps.

It wasn't until I started Khan Academy, though, that I realized the problem of equal-opportunity learning was even worse than I suspected. In much of the world, limited resources, inadequate infrastructure, and a shortage of skilled teachers create formidable barriers to learning. Places like sub-Saharan Africa and South Asia experience alarmingly low primary school completion rates, with countless children unable to attend school or forced to drop out due to poverty or conflicts. Also, in much of the world, deep-rooted discrimination toward girls and marginalized communities further hinders access to education. While millions of children every year are not going to school, girls are twice as likely to never set foot in a classroom.

The situation isn't much better when children have access to schools. A 2004 UNESCO study reported that 25 percent of teachers in India were absent from school, and only about half were teaching. Even when the teacher did show up, they had not received adequate training on the material.

These types of problems are not limited to the developing world. In the United States, children living in poverty enter kindergarten up to eighteen months behind their peers developmentally. This is likely due to a number of factors, including poor access to high-quality preschools and reading materials, as well as trouble securing tutoring to the degree that many middle- and upper-class families are able to.

Meanwhile, in many Asian countries, such as South Korea, China, Japan, and India, families often pay for their children to attend expensive after-school courses. This allows students to maintain an edge in an extremely competitive environment. These programs are expensive and exact an incredible mental health toll on children.

Clearly, education opportunities for children are, at best, uneven and suboptimal for most of the world. As Stanford University's Susanna Loeb knows, quality education is a powerful force for change, but sadly, not everyone has access to it. "We try to create more equitable and effective education systems, but we run into a lot of roadblocks," she tells me.

Loeb studies education policy and has spent her career as a professor of education trying to increase student access to learning materials and individualized instruction. The United States, for instance, has a decentralized education system. Administering uniform education to a country in which each school district makes its own decisions remains a near-impossible task. Loeb also cites increasing differences in achievement across unequal groups, especially students with special needs. Inequalities also exist in how kids do within groups. Most evident are low-income kids, or those from marginalized communities, who have not had access to the same educational opportunities as others. The schools in their neighborhoods are often underfunded, meaning they offer students limited extracurricular activities and fail to provide courses like advanced math or higher-level science. This problem becomes exponentially worse when you expand the scope internationally, in places with limited resources.

Educators have found short-term, narrow, and local solutions to some of these problems, but few provide the kind of equalizing force we want to be working toward in providing equal-access education globally. "The problem remains one of scaling, and that's where technology can be helpful," she says.

For the technology to be truly transformative, it has to be equitable. It can't increase the divide between rich and poor. It can't leave people behind.

This is why I started Khan Academy. The internet afforded us the ability to go directly to every classroom, every student, and every family in the world without having to necessarily navigate the same policy machinations faced by traditional reform efforts. The social return on investment is orders of magnitude more impactful. For example, our team operates on a budget equivalent to some high schools in the United States but reaches more than a hundred million learners a year around the world—and it has the potential to serve billions. We have aspired to be comprehensive, tackling all major academic subjects from pre-K to college. This allows us to not only raise the ceiling in existing classrooms but also to raise the floor for kids who do not have access to world-class schools or certain courses. I see our free online educational resources as having the potential to be part of the education safety net for the world.

This is not theoretical. Such was the case of a young woman named Sola, living in the Taliban heartland of Afghanistan, who was forbidden from going to school. Luckily, she had an internet connection and a supportive family. Khan Academy allowed her to teach herself everything from pre-algebra to biology, chemistry, physics, and calculus. She aspired to become a theoretical physics researcher in the United States, and through incredible determination and the help of others willing to give her a shot, she is now a quantum computing researcher at Tufts University and a published author.

Our team often hears stories along these lines, though we recognize that Sola's experience isn't typical. She was able to support herself in ways that most students are not capable. But what if the next ten million Solas have access to an army of tutors that can ensure that they stay motivated and engaged?

We know that if a well-trained tutor pulls kids out of class for thirty minutes a day, four days a week—a technique that Loeb refers to as high-dosage tutoring—there's really good evidence it produces a significant motivating effect for students no matter where they are.

However, we run into the issue of cost and scalability in wealthy and poor regions alike.

A lack of tutoring resources isn't the only barrier. Every student requires and deserves unique attention, and it is hard to provide different things to different students who need support and practice in their zone of proximal development, building on what they know and taking it to the next step.

This is where the work now finds us, as artificial intelligence continues to play a transformative role in bridging the global education divide and fostering equal-opportunity learning for all. With large language model applications that students can access with little more than a smartphone, we might eventually give students everywhere some, or even all, of the major pieces of a world-class education.*

"AI technology allows educators of varying levels of experience with a robust set of tools to create an environment that's conducive for learning," Loeb says. "Technology augments the motivation that a relationship with an adult gives them. All the evidence that we have to date says that students need personalized contact to remain motivated, an adult who they trust to give them materials to work with and celebrate successes, or support them when they are struggling."

---

* Roughly 65 percent of the global population has access to the internet (though this percentage varies widely among different countries and regions), and more than half the global population owns a smartphone.

ECONOMICS OF AI
IN EDUCATION

A decent education is expensive anywhere in the world. In the US, Louisiana spends roughly $10,000 per student per year; New York spends $40,000. In India, government schools might spend anywhere between $500 and $1,200 per student per year. Despite the range in resources, the fundamental model is the same. Students are moved lockstep through curricula, oftentimes feeling lost or bored. If a student doesn't keep pace in understanding a foundational concept, the class keeps moving. Limited support exists for personalization or for revisiting gaps, much less for one-on-one tutoring. This is despite the fact that many classrooms have students at a wide range of preparedness—some may be ahead of pace while others may be two or three grade levels behind.

The COVID-19 pandemic made things worse. During the 2020 school shutdowns, Black and Hispanic households with school-age children were 1.4 times as likely as white children to face limited access to computers and the internet, and more than two in five low-income households had only limited access. A bad prepandemic situation became downright dire. Consider that before 2020, 6 percent of Detroit eighth graders were performing at grade level; afterward, it dropped to 3 percent. The average American classroom in 2019 contained a spread of three grade levels of ability. After the pandemic, this spread expanded to six grade levels of ability. Put another way, in the same classroom of thirty students, teachers had to somehow support learners who were four-to-five grade levels behind while not boring the students who might have been ready to move ahead.

To address the situation, the US federal government funded $86 billion for elementary and secondary school emergency relief funds, amounting to $2,000 per American K–12 student. A lot of this money flowed into live tutoring programs, based on decades of research showing that tutoring can be an effective intervention for kids. Unfortunately, years later, most of the money was gone, with little to show for it. In hindsight, most experts believe this is because the tutoring was not connected to what was going on inside the classroom, and many students found it logistically hard to access. Students might have also run up against a stigma associated with going to tutoring in the first place.

A platform like Khanmigo exists to bridge this gap—offering personalized, accessible, and high-quality education. Even before Khanmigo, efficacy studies had shown that classrooms using Khan Academy as little as thirty to sixty minutes a week during the pandemic not only avoided the COVID slide but outperformed pre-COVID standards by 20 to 40 percent. And this didn't cost $2,000 per student. It was free.

Now, large language model platforms build off of those results to provide even richer support. An AI tutor is available whenever students need it, including in the classroom while they are doing their existing academic work. It can inform teachers and parents exactly what students are working on and where they need more help. Students who are further behind don't need to feel shame or embarrassment in asking for assistance, since the AI isn't a real person. Curious students can ask questions without feeling like they are wasting someone's time.

Providing scaled support like this is incredibly cost-effective and accessible, but it isn't free. Even before considering generative AI, our annual budget as a nonprofit is more than $70 million. That's a significant number, but it is also equivalent to the budget of a large high school in many parts of the United States—and Khan Academy reaches more than a hundred million learners a year. We need to raise a large chunk of this money every year from philanthropists to keep the content and software free to users. These resources are necessary for content development, product development, and server costs, among other things.

Generative AI adds a new layer of expenses beyond the cost of paying the salaries of engineers, designers, product managers, and content developers to iteratively improve a platform like Khanmigo. This is because the computation costs of a large language model like GPT-4 are significant. Right now, our best estimate of the computation costs of average usage of Khanmigo is between five and fifteen dollars a month per user. Assuming that we will have millions of users—which would cost tens of millions of dollars in computation costs—it is unlikely that we can raise enough money from philanthropy alone to offer the service for free. While dramatically cheaper than live tutoring, which can easily cost thirty dollars an hour, the platform does become less accessible than our free resources since we will need to charge school districts for access.

That said, between philanthropy and funding by local school districts, the cost to the students in those districts is, and will remain, free. However, this still doesn't address accessibility for poorer countries where thirty dollars a year could make up a significant portion of total education costs. The good news is that the computation will become cheaper and we will get better at using it more efficiently. These two trends should help bring the cost down by a factor of ten in the next few years. If we can reduce the costs by a factor of one hundred, which should happen in the next five to ten years, it will become comparable to the cost of using nongenerative web-based applications today.

At that point, the only real limits to access are the same ones we face with traditional Khan Academy: students would need access to the internet and devices, which aren't reliably available to everyone. Nevertheless, I am hopeful that between devices getting cheaper and providers like SpaceX's Starlink using swarms of satellites to provide low-cost broadband, nearly universal access will become a reality.

One major barrier to access in the early days of online learning was language. Now, large language models like GPT-4 can operate in every major language. Here, an English-language learner working on word problems in English could get support in his or her native language, or even in a mix of languages like Spanglish. The large language model's conversational abilities make it feel like a real-time interaction, fostering a sense of connection. Even more, it can be used to do much of the translation work of the core platform.

It is exactly that sense of connection and support that made finding a low-cost, multilingual, and scalable solution to bringing high-quality access to education across the globe so very vital, says Stanford's Susanna Loeb. "I'm optimistic and excited by what we can do now. In places where access to resources and pedagogies has been a real constraint, this technology can be transformational."

Part VIII

AI, ASSESSMENTS, AND ADMISSIONS

Not everything that can be counted counts, and not everything that counts can be counted.

—WILLIAM BRUCE CAMERON

Evaluation is creation: hear it, you creators! Evaluating is itself the most valuable treasure of all that we value. It is only through evaluation that value exists: and without evaluation the nut of existence would be hollow. Hear it, you creators!

—FRIEDRICH NIETZSCHE

THE FUTURE OF K–12 ASSESSMENTS

I t has become fashionable to bash standardized tests in the United States. Every state has "summative" assessments at the end of each school year to measure how students and schools are performing. People often criticize these tests for being too narrow—they primarily use multiple-choice questions that target a subset of what is actually important in life. This can create pressure for educators to similarly narrow their focus in the classroom.

That's not all, though. Others argue that these tests take time away from learning and are not really actionable. By the time the scores come in over the summer, or at the beginning of the following school year, kids have moved on to a new grade with a new teacher. In addition, students have very little incentive to care about showing their best work on a test that is not connected to their grades. Also, demographic differences in performance can lead to claims of bias against some groups or schools. As education has become more politically charged, the lack of transparency into what these tests actually assess makes people skeptical.

Let's take a step back, however. When people raise objections to standardized tests, I like to interrogate what part they don't like and whether they are throwing out the baby with the bathwater. If they are against assessments altogether, I ask them how we can get better at anything without measuring it. And if we are going to measure, standardizing that measurement is arguably fairer, since it applies the same standard to everyone (versus "unstandardized" assessment). If the issue is with the perceived narrowness of what these tests measure, wouldn't the answer be to broaden the scope of the assessments to make them richer rather than abandon them entirely? Likewise, if the critique is around actionability or transparency, couldn't we make the tests more actionable and transparent?

Most of all, even though standardized tests might be imperfect, does removing them really make things more or less equitable? If a school serving underrepresented groups doesn't know where and how their students may be falling behind, how can they begin to fix the problem? Is it somehow better for educators, students, and families to not know their gaps? Eventually, these deficits will surface regardless. This is likely to happen years later, in college or in the workforce, when it is much harder to fix after years of falling behind.

I'd rather think about how we can improve standardized tests rather than try to remove them entirely. Solutions have existed even before generative AI. Let's consider the critique that there isn't much that teachers can do with the standardized testing results. Well, if the assessments could feed into a software platform for personalized practice—for example, having students work on addressing different weak points based on the standardized testing data—the information becomes actionable. Over time, the personalized practice software would make sense of a student's previous assessments and provide that student with more targeted recommendations.

Khan Academy has, in fact, done this for some standardized tests for many years now. That is, we use standardized testing information to better differentiate practice in a classroom, improving student outcomes. In a study of more than three hundred thousand students using standardized test scores to inform personalized practice on our platform, "students who engaged . . . during the 2021–22 school year at the recommended dosage of 30+ minutes per week exceeded growth projections by 26% to 38%, depending on grade."

Continuous standardized assessments *while* students are learning also avoids taking away valuable instruction time. Every exercise on our platform is standardized, and we have millions of data points about how students from different grade levels and demographics perform on them. Rather than just having students take a traditional state summative test once or twice a year, they can regularly practice their skills on our platform. Educators can then use the generated data to measure student learning in a standardized way. This gives a more accurate and regular read on how a student is performing. That data then becomes actionable by driving student recommendations for further learning. This type of continuous assessment offers higher-quality data points on a much more regular basis. Where traditional standardized tests might cover fifty to one hundred questions once or twice a year, continuous assessments can glean this much information *every week* without them even feeling like a separate evaluation. This approach also addresses the issue with student motivation: you are more likely to care if your daily practice is also assessing you in a standardized way behind the scenes, as that work impacts your class progress and grades.

Much of the political angst over assessments and what is happening inside the classroom is due to external stakeholders like parents and politicians not being able to directly observe what students are experiencing. Instead, they rely on second- and thirdhand accounts, which might not be entirely accurate, or they fail to understand how high-level standards tangibly manifest in a test or classroom.

The lack of transparency and flexibility of traditional standardized assessment stems from both the expense of creating the assessment items and the fact that they must remain secure; if any of them leak, the entire assessment can become invalid. On the other hand, if you have easily accessible online platforms that adaptively assess from a large bank of items—think hundreds of thousands of questions—you can let more stakeholders try out the assessment whenever they want without undermining it. This is because an adaptive assessment will give every student a different sequence of questions based on how they performed on previous ones. It's unlikely that two students will ever see the same set of questions.

Generative AI holds the potential to help with all of this. Large language models aren't yet good enough to make high-quality assessment items completely on their own, but they can help a human question writer/reviewer become much more productive. Eventually, this will allow us to produce many more items with the same resources, enabling a new wave of even more transparent and accessible assessments.

This still leaves the question of how to deepen and broaden the skills that standardized assessments can measure. While multiple-choice or numeric-entry questions can get you pretty far when assessing some types of skills, they can't really capture how well you write, engage with a problem, or think creatively. Historically, these more nuanced tasks have been prohibitively expensive to assess widely. To gauge even basic open-ended questions, you need expert human reviewers working with complex rubrics and systems to ensure consistency. Richer assessments akin to a thesis defense for a PhD or a job interview have historically been impossible to do at scale.

This is about to change. The latest generation of large language models holds the potential to allow us to conduct this type of rich assessment economically and universally.

Consider reading comprehension: Today, students read a passage and then answer a few multiple-choice questions based on it. These questions might ask something about, say, the author's intent, followed by four choices. In the coming years, we will increasingly see assessments use generative AI to engage students about their views or the author's intent without the need for multiple choices. It will ask students to just write or speak their thoughts, and the AI will be able assess that response in a consistent way. Even better, it will be able to engage in a conversation with students about why they feel that way and discuss the evidence they are drawing on. The entire assessment will resemble a fluid, wide-ranging conversation with a thoughtful, empathetic, and fun mentor. Parts of it might involve role-playing or trying to work through a simulation. It wouldn't necessarily even have to be separate from learning. The same AI tutor that is there to help you would also build up evidence of what you know and don't know.

This goes beyond language and reading comprehension. In math, the AI can ask students to explain their reasoning or develop a proof. In science, it might assess how well a student can design an experiment or critique a research paper, arguably two of the most powerful elements to becoming a scientist. AI-driven simulations can assess student problem-solving skills. As AI takes on increasing visual capabilities, it will be able to critique and assess visual works, pictures, or videos of a presentation.

Of course, using AI for assessment can rightfully make folks wary. What if the AI has biases that are not immediately apparent? What if it makes mistakes? I try to compare this kind of hypothetical to the status quo. Current assessments are written by thoughtful but fallible human beings with their own biases. We already know that by not leveraging AI, we are limiting ourselves to a much narrower type of assessment that arguably magnifies a bias toward prioritizing easy-to-measure skills over ones that are harder to measure but perhaps more important. Historically, when we have been able to administer richer assessments, like in PhD oral thesis defenses or job interviews, they are inconsistent and rife with more bias than any current standardized exam. Generative AI allows us to capture the best of both worlds: standardization and scale with richness and nuance. Because of its potential accessibility, stakeholders will have a far easier time trying it out and auditing it themselves.

I am not saying that we should blindly assume that any AI assessment is going to be good. In fact, I am afraid a lot of people are going to create some very bad ones, rife with bias. I also believe, however, that with proper care, transparency, and guardrails, we can mitigate the risks and develop assessments that are far richer, more accurate, and fairer than those that we have today. This will have positive consequences for the education system as a whole, re-opening the aperture of what makes a quality education. By measuring skills long thought to be immeasurable, such as communication, creativity, and curiosity, it will naturally motivate the system to care a lot more about developing the whole person.

THE AI OF COLLEGE ADMISSIONS

The classic components considered in college admissions are grades, standardized tests, extracurriculars, essays, and letters of recommendation. AI will change how most if not all of these factors are valued, developed, and evaluated.

I've already argued that generative AI is going to transform schoolwork and grading in the classroom; students will be able to do much richer assignments, and teachers will have more support grading them. I've also discussed how standardized assessment is likely to change. Assessment will be deeper, much more continuous, and indistinct from learning. Over time, either standardized tests like SATs and ACTs will move in this direction, or new assessments will enter the space to take advantage of the opportunity.

Other than extracurriculars, the remaining components—essays and recommendations—both involve writing. This is the most obvious place where large language models introduce some very big ethical questions. Teachers and guidance counselors may use generative AI to write their recommendation letters. Students are likely to use large language models to generate impressive-sounding essays that misrepresent their actual writing ability or creativity. This poses a challenge for admissions officers to accurately evaluate the validity of applicants' work.

And yet heads of admissions at top universities tell me that the advent of generative AI has simply shined the spotlight on inequities that they have known about since long before large language models arrived. Take the Varsity Blues scandal, for example. This was a case in which wealthy celebrity parents paid hundreds of thousands of dollars to hire an unethical college admissions coach who not only wrote application essays but went as far as completely fabricating extracurricular activities, including photos. While this is an extreme example, an entire industry exists around college admissions coaches that only affluent families can afford. The going rate in Silicon Valley, where I live, is roughly four hundred dollars per hour for the top coaches. This can amount to tens of thousands of dollars to assist one student through a college admissions cycle. What do these coaches do? The more ethical ones advise students on how to approach extracurriculars and essay topics, help families think through good college options, and provide students with thoughtful feedback on early essay drafts. At the more unethical side of the spectrum, they might provide so much editing of a student's essay that they are essentially writing it for them. Either way, these affluent students receive significant help. Even if they do not hire a coach, many of these families have a lot of insider knowledge about the byzantine college admissions process and use it to give their children a leg up.

Tools like ChatGPT are obviously much more accessible to a broad group of people who never could have afforded high-priced college admissions coaches. And like these coaches, generative AI can be used for ethical and unethical purposes, as well as everything in between. It has now opened the door for everyone to play in the ethical gray area that was once only the domain of the affluent.

Something similar is likely to happen when it comes to recommendations. High-priced admissions coaches can't write recommendations, but guidance counselors and teachers serving wealthier students tend to have a lot more knowledge of how to give their students the best shot at university admission. Wealthier schools also tend to have smaller classes in which teachers and guidance counselors can get to know their students better and have more time to spend on each student's recommendation. Now someone writing a reference can work with generative AI tools to better express the strength of an applicant.

So, on the positive side, generative AI can help close the gap between the rich and poor. Now everyone—not just the affluent—needs to decide how much help is too much help. On the negative side, less-ethical students are likely to push the envelope, putting the more-ethical students at a disadvantage. Meanwhile, admission directors need to wrestle with whether this entire exercise of writing essays even still provides a credible signal for admissions.

To address that, it's worth questioning why essays and recommendations are part of admissions in the first place. In most countries, admission to highly selective universities is a fairly objective process. In India, entry to the hyperselective Indian Institutes of Technologies (IITs) is based solely on the Joint Entrance Exam (JEE). IITs admit the students with the top test scores, permitting quotas for some underrepresented groups. Not only do the highest scorers get their pick of IIT campuses, they also get to select their majors first. In India, this is a deliberate attempt to steer clear of the corruption that has often infected other institutions in the country.

Nothing remotely subjective like essays, recommendations, or extra-curriculars is involved.

On the other hand, admissions directors at highly selective universities in the United States will talk about subjective things like "building a community of diverse future leaders." Yes, they index on test scores and grades to some degree, but many of these institutions could fill their freshmen classes many times over with students who have perfect test scores and GPAs. Put another way, at some top schools, half of the applicant pool will have grades and test scores indicating that they could more than succeed academically if admitted, yet the university will only be able to admit 3–6 percent of them. This leads to a highly subjective process of trying to gauge the student's personality and backstory through essays, extracurriculars, and recommendations. Have the students overcome obstacles? Do they seem collaborative? Are they likely to make an impact on the world one day? These are big, deep questions to ask about young people who are seventeen or eighteen years old. I think many people are skeptical of how well admissions officers can judge these qualities based on some essays and recommendations that are subject to significant outside influence.

Extracurriculars are arguably a more tangible display of a student's leadership or commitment to community, but this, too, can be hard to judge. Did the student win the international science fair on their own? Is it a coincidence that their experiment studied heart disease and their mother is an academic cardiologist? Was that volunteer work really substantive or just something that sounds impressive?

This has all led to a randomness in American competitive college admissions that is clear to anyone who has been involved in the process. Many of the brightest, most collaborative, and poised people have been rejected far more than one might expect. The assumption is usually that they weren't sufficiently represented by glowing recommendations or unique essays. On the other hand, visit any highly selective college and you will meet many impressive young people. You are also likely to meet many who are struggling academically or do not seem to embody traits like humility, collaboration, or leadership. Most assume that these students were unusually good at constructing a paper narrative about themselves and gaming the system—or that their family was good at hiring someone who did this for them.

But what if we could have more standardized ways of evaluating "soft skills" like leadership, collaboration, empathy, and community service? Even better, what if this were coupled with ensuring deep academic competency? It turns out that this predates AI, but AI is going to take things to another level.

In 2020, I launched Schoolhouse.world to give anyone free, live tutoring via Zoom. This was more needed than ever, considering how many students were falling behind because of the COVID-19 pandemic. We have been able to keep it free by enlisting vetted volunteers to do the tutoring. The first step of the vetting process is to ensure the volunteers have mastery of the material they are going to tutor. They take the appropriate assessments while a separate tool records their face and screen. The volunteers have to explain their reasoning out loud. If they get at least a 90 percent on the assessment, the video is submitted for peer review. Assuming that everything looks good, they are allowed to start their tutoring journey, which still involves more vetting and training on the craft of tutoring itself. It's a rigorous method, ensuring quality tutors. After every tutoring session, students rate the volunteers. The volunteers have a transcript page that summarizes all the subjects they are certified in, the number of sessions they have run, their average rating, and any other qualitative feedback from the community that they'd like to highlight.

Jim Nondorf, the head of admissions at the University of Chicago, reached out to me soon after, asking if they could use the Schoolhouse.world tutor transcript for college admissions. His rationale was that any high school student who was a highly rated tutor for, say, calculus, surely knows the material well, especially considering our rigorous vetting process. Even more, if they have done many tutoring sessions and are highly rated, they are also likely to have strong leadership, communication, and empathy skills, not to mention their commitment to helping others by spending hours tutoring for free. We thought this was a great idea, and that fall, the University of Chicago made the Schoolhouse.world transcript an optional part of their application process. By the next admissions cycle, MIT had signed up as well. Fast-forward three years, and the list has grown to eighteen universities, including Yale, Brown, Caltech, Georgia Tech, and Columbia, with more added each year.

They all value the Schoolhouse.world transcript for the same reason that Jim Nondorf does: it is a dynamic and standardized way of measuring both subject-matter competency and communication, empathy, community service, and leadership. Unlike in the past, when admission officers didn't have a lot to go on if a student said that they did regular community service, on the Schoolhouse transcript, the extent and quality of their service is quantified in a standardized way. It is pretty much impossible to fake being a high-quality tutor over hundreds of sessions. Because of this, I learned during early conversations with several of these schools that students submitting these transcripts generally have a higher acceptance rate than the broader pool. A side benefit to all this is that it also provides a strong incentive for ambitious high schoolers to become tutors and help others.

How does AI play into this? First of all, Schoolhouse.world is already using AI to give volunteer tutors feedback on their tutoring sessions. The AI can "observe" Zoom sessions via the transcripts and give the tutors pointers on how they can improve. In the near future, it will give tutors real-time tips on how to serve their students better. Eventually, it will be able to provide narrative assessments of the tutor's style and capability on the Schoolhouse.world transcript, providing yet another rich input for admissions officers. Most important, the Schoolhouse.world example starts to point to how we can reimagine admissions altogether with AI.

Rather than essays or recommendations alone, what if the AI could do extensive text- or voice-based interviews with students, guidance counselors, and teachers? A protocol like ours could ensure that the interviewee is alone and not being fed answers by anyone. Eventually, the AI might make use of the video as well, which would be hard for a person to game. The interviewing AI would be aware of the student's grades, SAT/ACT scores, and extracurricular activities and then use that information to provide accurate references. Students could still submit essays and recommendations, but the AI could dig deep into interviewees to ensure that students authentically know what they are talking about.

Admissions interviews, typically conducted by alumni living in the same area as the student, are not conducted uniformly across all prospective students, and those that take place are incredibly inconsistent with one another. They can be useful for admissions officers to screen out applicants with obvious red flags, but they aren't super useful for comparing the bulk of students who all seem exceptional on paper. AI allows this process to become far more scalable, consistent, and auditable. In this context, the AI can consistently summarize its interactions and rate them in multiple dimensions based on a rubric created by the admissions office.

There is even the possibility that AI agents can vouch for the student themselves, just like a teacher who knows the student well. Think about it this way: an AI platform like Khanmigo has been working with you for some period of time. Whether you have used it for a month or for many years of schooling, it knows your strengths and your passions and can plausibly render a dynamic picture of who you are. When it is time to apply to college, the AI can write a recommendation letter for you. The letter is standardized across every student who uses the platform, only it has different memories based on its experiences with each learner. Imagine if everyone in the country had the same teacher. This teacher would actually be a pretty good arbiter. If we wanted to take this to the extreme—and it is not clear that we do—the AI recommender could talk to the AI interviewer on the admissions side to see if there is a good fit.

I know this raises fears of bias in both directions. There are some biases you want. You want the process to be biased toward thoughtful, collaborative young people who could be tomorrow's humble future leaders. You of course don't want it to be biased along lines of gender, race, religion, or geography. A 100 percent bias-free solution might be impossible, but that shouldn't be the hurdle. Instead, any AI system needs to be demonstrably better than the status quo, which usually involves all sorts of bias. This is not hypothetical. In a

2018 Supreme Court case, it was clearly established that Harvard admissions officers consistently rated Asian American applicants lower on personality traits, oftentimes arbitrarily overruling the observations of in-person interviewers. Harvard's admissions process scored applicants in five categories—"academic," "extracurricular," "athletic," "personal," and "overall"—ranking students from 1 to 6, with 1 being the best. White applicants got higher personal ratings than Asian Americans, with 21.3 percent of white applicants getting a 1 or 2 compared to 17.6 percent of Asian Americans. Alumni interviewers gave Asian Americans personal ratings comparable to those of white applicants, but the admissions office issued them the worst scores of any racial group.

It took a major lawsuit for this data to surface. Most of the time, the biases embedded in this very opaque process are well hidden. The power of an AI-based interviewer and assessor is that they can be audited. You can test them with identically qualified applicants with different demographics and publish the results to ensure consistency across race, gender, or background.

Rather than introducing new problems in college admissions, AI is forcing us to realize existing deficiencies while offering the possibility for positive change. Used thoughtfully, perhaps with a bit of educated bravery, it might enable us to move to a fairer and more transparent world.

Part IX

WORK AND WHAT COMES NEXT

The one who plants trees, knowing that he will never sit in their shade, has at least started to understand the meaning of life.

—RABINDRANATH TAGORE

Learn the rules like a pro, so you can break them like an artist.

—PABLO PICASSO

EMPLOYMENT IN AN AI WORLD

Many people fear that AI is going to lead to mass layoffs in favor of new, AI-powered tools that can do jobs faster, cheaper, and more efficiently than humans. Some companies have already paused hiring for roles that they think artificial intelligence will replace in the coming years. In 2023, IBM announced that it was suspending or slowing back-office hiring by 30 percent over a five-year period for jobs that could ultimately be done by AI. IBM's revelation suggests that the future of work is going to roll out differently, with back- or middle-office jobs disappearing, together with non-client-facing roles involving tasks such as creating budgets, managing data, completing office repairs, and organizing records. Reading the tea leaves, we can see where this might be going.

What will jobs in an AI-infused marketplace look like and how do we prepare our learners for them? Since ChatGPT came on the scene, many in the know have been saying that you won't get replaced by AI, but you might get replaced by someone else using AI.

Writers and copywriters using AI could potentially be three to five times as productive. The same will go for software engineers who are using AI copilots to debug and fill in large portions of their code. Graphic designers will be able to make fifty variations of a logo by tweaking a series of text-based prompts. Given this increase in productivity, are we going to need as many copywriters, engineers, and graphic designers?

I suspect it will be a mixed bag. Because we are at such a technological inflection point that allows us to do so much more with generative AI, the demand for engineers, especially ones who are five to ten times more productive, is only going to go up. We've seen this happen in the past. In the early 2000s, accelerating globalization allowed a lot of software engineering work to be outsourced to places such as India. As a young engineer at the time, I thought I had to go to business school and change to a career in finance to avoid being disrupted by low-cost labor from abroad.

I was wrong. Since then, software engineering salaries have gone up much faster than the rate of inflation. This is because smartphones and the rise of the internet created an environment conducive to new software-based solutions. Generative AI is creating an even riper environment for further innovation. From my vantage point, because of generative AI, there is endless work for engineers who can creatively apply these technologies to solve new problems in nearly every industry.

On the other hand, I'm not as bullish for, say, the people currently writing news summaries about daily stock market fluctuations. If it isn't already happening, these types of tasks will soon be done by generative AI. The copywriters and technical writers who are going to survive are going to be the ones who lean in most on AI to increase their productivity. The other 90 percent are going to have to find something else to do.

The good news is, generative AI will require new kinds of work.

One of the hottest jobs today is being a prompt writer or prompt engineer. Two years ago, no one knew what those jobs were. It turns out that an open-minded and creative copywriter could transition quite well into some of these roles. Generative AI is also making us envision entirely new opportunities around safety, security, and antibias. I suspect that as more organizations wrestle with how to apply this technology, new opportunities will continue to emerge.

In the same way that teachers are using AI to facilitate their more rote or mundane responsibilities, positions from HR to management will begin to task AI with producing hiring letters or meeting reports. On the surface, this sounds good and helpful, yet I also can't help but consider the larger consequences.

It isn't just about individual jobs. AI-induced natural selection is also going to be happening at the corporate level. If we have two companies—one that's smaller, leaner, and more automated, and another that's bigger, slower, and more dependent on human labor—over time, the smaller company will be able to offer an equivalent or better product for a lower price and start to gain more market share from the bigger company, which ultimately leads to a net loss of jobs. This is a common trend that we see in many industries, and this will continue as automation and technology advance at a rapid pace. On the one hand, the smaller company can provide goods or services more efficiently and at a lower cost, which can be beneficial for consumers. On the other hand, the job losses can be difficult for those who are directly affected.

This is already starting to unfold in dramatic fashion. In 2006, the education technology company Chegg, Inc. launched as a service that assisted nearly three million customers with homework, digital and physical textbook rentals, and online tutoring. Just two and a half years before ChatGPT, *Forbes* called the company the most valuable ed-tech business in America. Once ChatGPT arrived, Chegg pivoted and began to incorporate AI into its platform, but it was no match for ChatGPT. When Chegg announced its quarterly earnings in May 2023, the CEO admitted that the service had been struggling to keep up with OpenAI's offering, because so many students were using the large language model for help with their homework. The company admitted it no longer had any idea how much money it was going to make that year because of the influence of ChatGPT. This bombshell admission led to Chegg's stock plummeting almost 50 percent. Since the arrival of generative AI, many have worried that these tools will upend established businesses. As distant as this fear once was, it remained speculative until it suddenly became a bit too real, with stories like this.

These sentiments are not mine alone.

"It's going to affect every industry differently, every person differently, and every job differently," Wharton's Ethan Mollick says. "The job that's least affected by AI, according to the early-stage research we have, is roofing, and yet I've talked to a couple roofers who're like, 'Actually, roofing is going to change, too, because we can now do all of our proposals with AI help.'"

When you develop artificial intelligence that can understand language, recognize patterns, and solve problems, as well as AI that can diagnose illnesses, make stock market trades, compose music, fight lawsuits, understand emotions, analyze genetic code, handle insurance claims, spray pesticides, engineer, and write articles, it is not hard to believe that more changes are coming. The successful strategy will not be to resist but to adapt.

HOW TO PREPARE KIDS TO THRIVE IN THE AI-FUTURE WORKPLACE

t is several months before we launch Khanmigo, and I am speaking at the Stanford Computer Science Department along with a professor named Chris Piech. He tells me a story about a young Stanford student he was advising who came into his office. "She was really upset, saying how she just learned how to code and now artificial intelligence was able to do it better," Piech says. "She felt like she was already marginalized."

For the past twenty years, software engineering and data science have been the hottest two jobs for young people right out of college. We encourage them to go into these professions if they want to be part of the future. We advocate for students to learn how to code to become part of the digital economy. But what we now know is that generative AI can do this well.

This creates tension. We are afraid to allow kids to use AI tools in school in order to prevent cheating, despite the fact that they will have future jobs requiring close symbiosis with these same tools.

This is compounded by what Bill Gates calls another "confounding paradox." We now have a tool that makes it easier for those who want to learn, but sadly, in some cases, it makes people wonder if they need those skills at all. Why should students learn skills that AI can do better?

"So what did you tell her?" I ask Piech.

"I said I believe the ability to code is going to be really important. I told her if she wants to create any type of major solution, including a solution that uses generative AI, even if the generative AI can write pieces of code, you really need to know how those pieces can fit together."

In other words, he says, it will be important to learn to work in concert with generative AI. In order to build anything, you are still going to need to know how the pieces fit together and how they actually work.

Entry-level employees who understand AI, and use it, will be far more efficient than those who don't. My fourteen-year-old son loves to code and aspires to someday make video games. I think he has a great shot at this, but I also encourage him to use generative AI to tackle more ambitious projects than he would ordinarily be able to do on his own. He is going to be able to make games that, before generative AI, would have required a team of half a dozen professional engineers to create.

It is well documented that generative AI can write with real competency. This does not mean that one should not learn how to write. If one of my children came to me and said they wanted to be a screenwriter, I would tell them to get really good at writing screenplays. Then I would encourage them to use generative AI to take on more and more enterprising projects. You need to be good at a craft in order to know what high quality looks like. Even more, an individual with a strong sense of story and film will no longer have to stop at the screenwriting phase. A screenwriter could actually produce the movie with the help of generative AI. This technology can already produce music and videos. It can even edit raw footage. A film that used to cost a hundred million dollars and take several years to make will likely soon be doable by a handful of film students with a fraction of that budget. We do not know how much better these systems are going to get, but even the current generation of AI is starting to cause a disruption along these lines in the film industry, as well as in many others.

Early controlled studies on productivity improvement due to AI by the Wharton School are seeing 30 to 80 percent performance improvement on many high-powered white-collar analytical tasks. This includes stronger and more concise writing, analysis, consulting, and programming.

"If you want to be in these fields, AI is, and will remain, a part of your life," Mollick says. "You need to figure out if you can use AI to be ten times more productive—meaning there remains a need for humans to be in the loop. If you are trying to be a copy editor, a coder, or even a roofer, you will need to be a centaur, only instead of being half human and half horse, you must be half human and half large language model."

To meet the demands of this new world of work, educators are going to have to, explicitly or implicitly, continue making their students familiar with these tools and the power that they have. Generative AI is what's called a general-purpose technology, one that comes along very rarely. Think of the transformations brought about by steam power, computers, or the internet. Generative AI is likely to transform our lives faster, and more profoundly, than any of these previous inflection points.

The Industrial Revolution was all about specialization of labor. We created assembly lines and workers then specialized in certain jobs on that assembly line. That trend has continued ever since, as complex organizations have developed complex systems. The benefits of specialization are going to continue in an AI world.

"Exactly what the job market of tomorrow looks like is very hard to predict, but the deeper the skill set, whether it's medical consultation, scientific thinking, or customer support, the more value it's going to have, even in a world where productivity will be enhanced by AI," Bill Gates tells me. Not only is there more reason than ever for kids to continue to learn about their fields of interest, he says, but students need to *accelerate* learning these skills, and to learn them as well as possible. "Entry-level jobs are going to require people to understand how to use large language models and all of the tools they offer. You'll need them to create everything from invoices to business plans. The workplace is going to encourage its workforce to come up with the best product it can. The higher your skill level is, the more your skill will retain a substantial value in the workforce. It's the workforce *plus* the AI, working together."

Yet, in the world we are entering, it is not just about specialization. Those who succeed might be deep in one or two areas, but they also need entrepreneurial expertise in a broad set of domains in order to put all of the pieces together.

This is nothing new. When I started Khan Academy, I knew how to code, so I was able to start prototyping it without needing any money or help. I was also good at putting together tools that already existed and seeing utility in them that others did not. I used YouTube for videos and instant messaging to communicate with the cousins I was tutoring. I was a hedge fund analyst, so even though I had never run a nonprofit before, I knew enough about finance and accounting to get it off the ground. People who are able to embark on a project this way will always have an advantage as entrepreneurs, but there is a limit to how far they can go on their own. At some point, they need to raise money and hire people. Just as software and the internet facilitated remarkable growth (I was able to scale Khan Academy to one hundred thousand users as a side hobby on my own), generative AI will allow the next generation of entrepreneurs to go even further.

We are entering a world where we are going back to a pre-Industrial Revolution, craftsmanlike experience. A small group of people who understand engineering, sales, marketing, finance, and design are going to be able to manage armies of generative AI and put all of these pieces together.

When economists talk about the factors of production, they talk about things like capital, labor, land, and other resources such as energy. But they also talk about entrepreneurship. From an economics point of view, entrepreneurship is really the creativity of knowing how to put resources together in order to create value. So how do we prepare every student to be this type of entrepreneur?

Step one is to get out of the way. I believe all human beings are born highly creative and entrepreneurial. Unfortunately, our Industrial Revolution–designed education system unintentionally suppresses both traits. Kids learn to sit in rows, make no noise, and take notes. They are spoon-fed knowledge and forced to learn in lockstep. Both academically and socially, nonconformity is punished. When students are young adults and most capable of being creative entrepreneurs, the system instead bogs them down with hours of busywork that squeezes out any time for their passions.

Step two is a little bit more traditional. As Bill Gates mentioned, the successful workers of the future will be those with deep and broad skills. The "three Rs" of reading, writing, and arithmetic are more important than ever. On top of that, a solid appreciation and understanding of history, art, science, law, and finance would round out someone well. Luckily, we now have the technological tools to ensure the mastery of these skills without having to enforce the lock-step learning of the industrial age.

Finally, it's more important than ever that students have strong communication, collaboration, and empathy skills. Traditional en-trepreneurship tends to invoke ideas of starting a business, but what I am describing goes much further and includes a more *personal* vi-sion. It is an ability to look at the various parts of your job, and to see any problem that needs solving, to know where you must focus your research and to understand the pieces that you need to put in place in order to solve it. To thrive in an AI world, everyone needs to be this type of entrepreneur, even if they are working for someone else. Schools can make this happen by putting students in the driver's seat more often, using AI tools to better support student mastery of core skills and free up time for student agency and creativity.

MATCHMAKING BETWEEN JOB SEEKERS AND EMPLOYERS

I n 1999, for a cover story on the new millennium, *Computerworld* magazine asked me for predictions that might come to pass in the coming ten to twenty years. I was surprised that they were asking me, a recent college graduate who was a new product manager at Oracle, given that the other nineteen people they interviewed were titans of technology like Bill Gates and Larry Ellison. The editor in chief had attended my college graduation, where I spoke as class president; he thought it would be interesting to get a more youthful perspective in the mix.

Regardless, I didn't want to waste the opportunity and ran with the most far-out ideas that I thought might be plausible. I talked about a future in which we would all have artificially intelligent personal agents to represent us in "cyberspace." The agents would purchase things for you and broker transactions, even matchmake between employers and employees (or romantic partners). Twenty-three years went by and, for the most part, my predictions didn't come to pass. AI hadn't advanced to the necessary degree.

Fast-forward to now, and this latest generation of generative AI holds the very real promise of making my predictions seem conservative. As optimistic as I was about progress in AI in 1999, what we have started to see in the early 2020s far surpasses anything that I could have imagined happening in my lifetime. Among many other things, AI, as our personal agent, will soon post, find, apply for, and even acquire jobs for us.

Traditionally, for every job opening at our company, we write job descriptions. Today, a hiring manager must first take the time to write that job description or work alongside someone in HR to create it. Once we post a job, we typically get several hundred résumés for every opening. Then we have our talent acquisition team go through those résumés, which is incredibly tedious work. Because these screeners can realistically spend only a few seconds on each résumé, their eyes likely focus on things like name brands of previous employers, keywords in previous job titles, or degrees from well-known universities. I can imagine that sometimes they are in the mood to dig a bit deeper, but sometimes they aren't. And this is before we come to any personal biases they bring to the table. This process is likely to miss a lot of great applicants, especially those who didn't spend time at well-known companies or schools.

Regardless, our recruiters flag a small pool of candidates for phone screens and possibly more interviews. If they pass the thirty-minute phone screen based on the recruiter's subjective judgment, the candidate will then be interviewed by four to six team members in the function that they are applying for. Due to scheduling complexity, this takes days or weeks. It's also quite expensive: six one-hour interviews from team members who make the equivalent of one hundred dollars an hour costs us six hundred dollars, before even considering the time to prep and debrief. To avoid inconsistency, we give interviewers a framework of questions. Yet, at the end of the day, the preferences and the mood of the interviewer likely dictate where the conversation goes. Eventually, we hope to get a signal that we have found a top choice and cross our fingers that we are making a good hire. It is a similar process almost everywhere.

This is an imperfect process on both sides. We probably overlooked some great candidates, and it took a lot of time and energy to eventually make an offer, knowing that it may not even be a perfect match. On top of that, by its very nature the process was not completely consistent. I also wouldn't be surprised if people's personal biases tilted things for or against certain applicants based on things that were not relevant to the job.

If all parties had infinite time and energy, the recruiters and the hiring managers would engage in in-depth conversations with every person interested in that job. They would apply the same standard consistently and be in the same mood and have the same level of enthusiasm for every candidate. Even better, we would be able to audit this process for bias by running test candidates through it. On top of that, in an ideal world it would take hours—not days or weeks—to come to a decision.

This might seem unrealistic, but it may now very well be possible to approach this ideal.

Large language models can already streamline the standard process in fairly obvious ways. Recruiters can use them to help draft job posts and interview questions. Candidates can use them to create cover letters and résumés. This, however, is just the tip of the iceberg.

In the future, if you are looking for a job, an application leveraging a large language model will create an interactive résumé that communicates with the AI that has posted the job you are applying for. Instead of just submitting a résumé and a cover letter into a void, *every* job candidate might be able to automatically have a rich conversation with the AI recruiter, an experience that potentially gives each person a much fairer shot.

You will not even have to wait for the employer's bot to schedule time with you. Rather, the employer's recruiter bot can talk to your agent bot. This agent will have learned to represent you accurately based on your employment history and extensive interviews that it has conducted with you.

Because it has been with you since you were a student, and because you've given it permission to access your entire work and education history, your skill sets, your interests, and even work samples you have produced, it will ask you what you are looking for in a job and the types of roles you might like to explore. It can even help coach you to think through career and education possibilities that match your life goals. Consider it as a supercharged life coach that learns to represent you to potential employers.

From there, it will look for the right positions on your behalf by talking to other AI bots that have posted these jobs. As a job seeker, your AI job agent could read literally every job posting that is out there. If you are looking to switch careers but do not have the right experience that 99 percent of employers want, your AI job agent could find the 1 percent willing to give you a shot. Your AI job agent might then report back that it just talked to a thousand employers and found a number that really value the fact that you are an outsider. Imagine a generative artificial intelligence that can solicit people over LinkedIn and reply to you with opportunities.

These bots, in theory, can have infinite conversations with each other and eventually glean a signal about a best fit for both parties. At the end of the day, if I am the hiring manager, my AI recruiting assistant will offer me the top five to ten people it thinks I should talk to based on the simulated conversations it has had with all the candidates' AI agents.

This isn't limited to just screening candidates. The AI recruiting assistant will be capable of engaging with the references that the candidate has provided. Based on this, it can further refine its recommendations.

Even during the live interview with the candidate, the AI recruiting assistant could whisper into your ear good follow-up questions or provide real-time feedback to ensure that you're interviewing as fairly and consistently as possible.

The job application and hiring process will become far more equitable, faster, and less resource-intensive for everyone. Each person, or at least their AI agent, gets an interview with the hiring AI. Every company gets a chance to get to know you through your AI agent. They will go through your entire job history. I can imagine a world in which the traditional résumé may no longer be relevant or useful because your AI agent will do a much better job of representing you.

It's worth acknowledging that this might make some people uneasy. In fact, one of the biggest fears around AI is the bias it might introduce while screening résumés or interviewing candidates. I'll be the first to admit that it will be near impossible to create a system that is free of bias. Yet I'd argue that AI will be an improvement when it can be demonstrably less biased and more consistent than the status quo, which is subjective and full of bias. Yes, we should heavily scrutinize any AI systems that claim they can assist in the recruiting process, but I also think that eventually you will have the tools that have not only made the process more inclusive and efficient but have also made it far less biased.

WHERE THIS LEAVES US AND WHERE IT WILL TAKE US: A CALL FOR EDUCATED BRAVERY

have a confession. I once thought I would be an AI researcher. I viewed, and still view, intelligence and perception—which are two different things—as the biggest mysteries of the universe. I was fascinated by the idea of being able to build something as smart, or even smarter, than any of us. I had read nearly every science-fiction book on the topic. I loved thinking about how we could prove whether another being was truly sentient. After all, we can only directly perceive our own perception. It is really a leap of faith that other creatures—including other people in our life—are truly sentient versus just acting like they are. The best way to understand intelligence, I once thought, was to construct machines that are capable of it.

When I was a freshman at MIT in 1994, I was lucky to have direct access to several of the titans of AI at the time. I sought out Patrick Henry Winston to be my freshman adviser. He was the director of the MIT Artificial Intelligence Laboratory and author of the canonical textbook on artificial intelligence at the time. I took his class, Introduction to Artificial Intelligence. I also took Marvin Minsky's class, Society of Mind. Minsky was Winston's mentor and the founder of the Artificial Intelligence Laboratory. He also won computer science's highest award—the Turing Award—for "his central role in creating, shaping, promoting, and advancing the field of Artificial Intelligence." His ideas were considered foundational for the field of artificial neural networks. He was also the AI adviser to Stanley Kubrick when he made perhaps the most famous AI film of all time, *2001: A Space Odyssey.*

These professors were incredibly intelligent, creative, and inspiring, but I found myself disappointed in where the field was and how slowly it seemed to be developing. The most impressive AI systems that could play games like chess were just good at anticipating decisions several moves ahead. No matter how proficient these systems got, no one really believed that they would be intelligent in the same way we are. Artificial neural nets were compelling from a philosophical point of view, but they weren't really capable of doing anything truly mind-blowing at the time. There hadn't been any big, new ideas in twenty or thirty years. Little did I know that this was the tail end of what would later be considered an "AI winter" among researchers.

So I decided to move on. I still loved computer science and thought that I would eventually try to start some type of tech company. But questions around intelligence and, by extension, education continued to draw me in because they seemed so fundamental to the advancing of society. The summer after my junior year, I received a fellowship to create software that allows students to learn and practice math at their own time and pace. Sound familiar?

I started to believe that people had a lot of latent, unused potential. For every person born with the raw material to be Albert Einstein or Marie Curie, how many get the education and support to do so? What if, with broader, more accessible education, we could increase by a factor of ten or one hundred the number of people capable of making the next major scientific, artistic, or entrepreneurial leap for us all? How many more diseases might we cure? How much faster might we explore the cosmos?

My curiosity wasn't just about fostering genius. If everyone had access to truly great education, I wondered, how many more billions of people might attain purpose and meaning in their lives?

But practical reality was there in the background. I grew up in a single-mother household. My parents separated shortly after I was born, and I only met my father once before he died when I was fourteen. He was a pediatrician and came from a prominent family of politicians and academics in Bangladesh, but we never received any financial support because I think he was barely making it himself. When he died, my sister and I inherited a Nissan Sentra that had more debt on it than it was worth. The only narrative I can piece together is that he and my mother were wildly incompatible, as they had an arranged marriage, and he likely suffered from depression. For most of my life, my mother was a cashier at various convenience stores, making enough money to be slightly below the poverty line. MIT was generous with financial aid, but I still had about thirty thousand dollars in debt upon graduation. The tech boom was heating up, and when I found out that I could make eighty thousand dollars a year as a new computer science graduate, which was about five times what my mother was making, I could not pass the opportunity by and took a job at Oracle Corporation.

I later went to business school and found myself as an analyst at a hedge fund. My then fiancée and now wife would give me grief about how I wasn't doing anything helpful for humanity with my talents and education. I found investing to be intellectually fascinating, though. It allowed me to study how the world worked, along with the animal spirits of the market. I also needed the money. I had further debt to pay from business school. I also knew that I was going to support my mother and other family members, and I was pretty determined to not perpetuate the financial insecurity that I grew up with. If I'm honest, I'm still more insecure about this than most of my friends. I would also tell folks that I was only going to do this until I was independently wealthy so that I could start a school on my own terms. I had some ideas about one day being the Dumbledore at a school that focused on putting students at the center and giving much more time and space for them to explore their passions.

It was at that time, in 2004, when I had family from New Orleans visiting me in Boston after my wedding. It came out of a conversation with my aunt that my twelve-year-old cousin Nadia was having trouble in math, and I offered to tutor her remotely. That led to the beginning of Khan Academy, which at its essence has been all about trying to scale the type of personalized learning that I did with Nadia to hundreds of millions of learners, across subjects, grades, and geographies.

Through the years, many people have asked me why I set up Khan Academy as a nonprofit. After all, my previous career was very for-profit, and I live in the middle of Silicon Valley, where scalable tech-enabled solutions can be worth a lot of money. Many have been skeptical whether a nonprofit could even compete with for-profit companies. There were two notions I couldn't get out of my head, however. First, I tend to believe in market forces, but there are a few sectors—namely, education and health care—where the outcomes of market forces don't always align with our values. Education and health care are two areas where our shared values tell us that, ideally, family resources shouldn't be a limiting factor in accessing the best possible opportunities. Most of us believe that every mind and life deserves to reach its full potential.

The second notion was more grandiose, if not outright delusional. One of my favorite sets of books is the Foundation series by Isaac Asimov. It takes place tens of thousands of years in the future, when humanity has colonized the galaxy, unified under one empire. Within that empire, an academic by the name of Hari Seldon has developed a new field called psychohistory—something of a combination of history, economics, and statistics—that can probabilistically predict large-scale historic trends. This science tells him that the Galactic Empire will enter a ten-thousand-year dark age within the next few hundred years. This will be ten thousand years of war, famine, and lost knowledge. His calculations show that nothing can prevent the coming dark ages, but it can be shortened. So he starts a foundation at the periphery of the galaxy to preserve knowledge and technology, which can then be used to shorten the coming chaos to "only" one thousand years. The book series mainly focuses on how the ensuing hundreds of years actually play out.

When I first read the Foundation series in middle school, I found it inspiring to think along those time scales. It was also the first moment I truly appreciated that the strength of a civilization doesn't lie in its physical size, power, and wealth. Those are just by-products of where the real strength lies: a society's culture, know-how, and mindset.

Jump ahead to when Khan Academy was beginning, and I

realized that very few people in our society think on a scale of more than a few years or decades, much less hundreds or thousands of years. Beyond this, the internet was clearly the transformational technology of our time, but no real institutions were being built with it. I began to wonder whether Khan Academy might just be able to become one of the first of them; something that could help educate billions of people for hundreds of years to come. It would be like Hari Seldon's foundation, except in our case, we could uplift humanity so that the present moment would feel like a dark age when looked back upon from fifty or a hundred years in the future. We only have one life—why not swing for the fences?

As Khan Academy grew and scaled from tens to hundreds of millions of people, that dream seemed to feel less and less delusional. Amazing people came out of the woodwork to help us. By the fall of 2009, I had quit my hedge fund job to work on Khan Academy full time. Ten months later, my family was quickly depleting our savings. Our first child was born, and I was having trouble sleeping because of financial stress and, to some degree, the shame of giving up a lucrative job for something that didn't seem to have a future. At what seemed like Khan Academy's darkest moment, Ann Doerr—who is now our chairperson—and John Doerr miraculously showed up and donated enough money for me to keep going. Since then, hundreds of thousands of people have donated to support us. Despite being a nonprofit, we have been able to build a team that rivals those of the most resource-rich tech companies. Hundreds of incredibly talented people have committed a major part of their careers to be part of the Khan Academy team, often taking considerable pay cuts to do so. Thousands of volunteers all over the world have now translated Khan Academy into over fifty languages. Inspirational leaders like

Bill Gates, Reed Hastings, and Elon Musk have become some of our biggest supporters and advocates. This journey seems so serendipitous that it has become something of an inside joke among the Khan Academy team that perhaps benevolent aliens are helping us so that, through education, we can prepare humanity for first contact.

This narrative seemed to be reinforced when Sam Altman and Greg Brockman of OpenAI reached out to us before anyone else with a technology that seemed to tie together every thread of my journey. GPT-4 was built on years of important innovations from many people and companies, but it was the first AI technology that truly made me wonder whether I was dreaming (or perhaps living in a simulation). It surpassed anything that, back in 1994, aspiring AI researcher Sal could have ever imagined happening in his lifetime. More important, it was the potential missing piece to our goal of delivering a truly world-class education for anyone, anywhere. I realized that as thrilling as it would be to be an AI researcher now, it was even more exciting to think about how the technology could be applied to help human potential.

This is not something to be taken lightly; there is real urgency here. Despite making us far more productive as a whole, this technology also has the potential to displace or disrupt many industries and jobs. The traditional labor pyramid—with less-skilled manual labor forming the bottom layer, bureaucratic white-collar jobs making up the middle layer, and highly skilled knowledge work and entrepreneurship making up the top—no longer applies. Robotics, including self-driving cars and trucks, is going to dramatically reduce the need for humans in that bottom layer. Generative AI can clearly perform large aspects of the work of the middle, white-collar layer and even parts of today's most skilled professions. A society in which all the productivity and resulting wealth accrues to only the tippy-top of the traditional labor pyramid, likely concentrated in Silicon Valley, with many others out of work, will not be a stable one. It might lead to massive wealth redistribution efforts. This scenario is dystopian because most people aren't looking for a handout. Rather, they want to have a sense of purpose and a feeling of contributing to the world.

The real solution is to invert that labor pyramid so that most people can operate at the top and use AI and other technology for their own productivity and entrepreneurship. The only way we have a hope of doing this is to use the same AI technology to lift the skills of a large chunk of humanity in the coming decades.

Few people may view the *Star Trek* universe through an economic lens, but doing so provides a window into a world that might soon be upon us. All of classical economics is based on the notion of scarcity—namely, that there isn't usually enough of anything to give everyone everything they want or need. Because of that, we use markets and pricing to allocate those goods, services, and resources to where they might result in the highest benefit. In *Star Trek*, however, there isn't much scarcity. Technology has allowed that society to replicate any food they want, transport themselves thousands of miles in the blink of an eye, communicate over light-years, and travel among the stars. All of humanity in that world has been fully educated so that they can participate in this bounty. Everyone is an explorer, researcher, engineer, artist, doctor, or counselor. Generative AI has the potential to allow many dimensions of our own society to be similarly low scarcity or highly abundant. Do we have the will to take us to the utopia of *Star Trek*?

If we don't, societies will increasingly fall prey to populism. People with time but no sense of purpose or meaning don't tend to be good for themselves or others. They are susceptible to the ideas of demagogues. Generative AI can be used to move us in this negative direction by reinforcing "fake news" with fabricated videos and images. It can be used by governments to police their own populations much more tightly than anything George Orwell imagined in *1984*. For decades it has been possible to put cameras and sensors throughout a city and to tap phone lines, but it was difficult to monitor all the information and make sense of it. AI could soon flag any recording or observation that seems like disobedience to the eyes of the state. Big Brother will not only be watching but will also have comprehension.

Without proper countermeasures and AI literacy, people will also fall victim to increasingly sophisticated fraud. In the near future, expect to get phone calls, or even video chats, from something that looks like your family member, telling you that they are in an emergency and that you need to wire them money.

AI will increasingly play a role in national security. Foreign enemies will have the capability to orchestrate increasingly sophisticated attacks on infrastructure using this technology—attacks that potentially involve manipulating human beings. AI-generated images of people waiting in line to get their deposits could go viral on social media and start a run on banks. State and nonstate actors will use generative AI within social media to try to influence the outcomes of our elections and make us more divided as a society. The best tacticians in the battles of the future are likely to be AI, not human.

These very real possibilities may motivate some to advocate for slowing down innovation. Honestly, even I find the pace of its development dizzying. But the genie is out of the bottle, and the bad actors are not about to slow down because we want them to. Today, the good actors have the edge, but it really is a race. The countermeasure for every risk is not slowing down; it is ensuring that those favoring liberty and empowering humanity have better AI than those on the side of chaos and despotism.

This moment can be an existential risk or an existential opportunity for us. People have every right to be both scared and hopeful of what this leap in technology and innovation means. I do not, however, think our fate is subject to the flip of a coin. Rather, each of us is an active participant in the decision about how we will use AI moving forward. If we act with fear, the rule followers might pause, but the rule breakers, from totalitarian governments to criminal organizations, are going to accelerate their development of AI. The only way that we can ensure that we are closer to reaching a utopian *Star Trek* scenario is if we double down our efforts on using large language models for the good of society.

This is not a drill: generative AI is here to stay. The AI tsunami has drawn back from the shore, and it is now barreling toward us. Faced with the choice between running from it or riding it, I believe in jumping in with both feet, while taking proper precautions so that we don't get hit with the flotsam.

Each of us has an obligation to make sure that we use this technology responsibly. This means that as developers we must put the necessary guardrails on it to protect our children. When problems arise, we should apply reasonable regulations, regulations that don't give an edge to rule breakers. All the while, we must accelerate our efforts and make sure that we are developing the technology with the right intent and the right pedagogy. This will allow us to accelerate the improvement of human purpose and potential. Let's use AI to create a new golden age for humanity, a time that will make today look like a dark age. From my vantage point, nothing could be more inspiring and important than that.

Acknowledgments

Thank you to Umaima Marvi for being the best life partner, whose support has been instrumental in every step of this journey.

Imran, Diya, and Azad, who inspire me every day to try to make myself and the world a little bit better. Masooda Khan, for raising me as a single mother and teaching me to persist when things get tough. Farah Khan, for being my first teacher and mentor. Naseem Marvi, for being an amazing mother-in-law, listener, and friend. Polly, for being the ideal foot warmer during much of the book-writing process.

Nadia, Arman, Ali, Azad, and Nazrat Rahman, for helping to plant the seed for all this. Dan Wohl, for being a great boss and mentor who was cool with me working on Khan Academy on the side while working for him.

Ann (our board chair) and John Doerr for believing in and supporting this effort from the beginning.

Shantanu Sinha, Ben Kamens, Jason Rosoff, and Bilal Musharraf, Khan Academy's first team beyond me that helped turn it into a real organization.

ACKNOWLEDGMENTS

Bill Gates, Jorge Paulo and Susanna Lemann, Carlos Rodriguez-Pastor, Reed Hastings, Dan Benton, Scott Cook, Signe Ostby, Ratan Tata, Carlos Slim, Tony Slim, Eric Schmidt, Elon Musk, David Siegel, Laura Overdeck, John Overdeck, Laurene Powell Jobs, David Stiles Nicholson, Carlyse Ciocca, Erica and Feroz Dewan, Ray and Barbara Dalio, Bob Hughes, Jack Little, Jeanne O'Keefe, Craig Santos, Charles, Liz, Chase, and Elizabeth Koch, Brian Hooks, Janine and Jeff Yass, Ravenel Curry, Laure and Guillaume Pousaz, Ross Annable, Lonnie Smith, Mark and Debra Leslie, Chuck Kung and Lisa Guerra, Larry Cohen, Sundar Pichai, James Manyika, Satya Nadella, Shantanu Narayen, Dharmesh Shah, Jack Dorsey, Jeb Bush, Sean O'Sullivan, Ted Mitchell, Patricia Levesque, Curtis Feeny, Sanjiv Yajnik, Fareed Zakaria, Arne Duncan, Tom Friedman, Diane Greene, Walter Isaacson, Todd Rose, David Coleman, Sameer Sampat, Dianne Seeman, Yuri Milner, Henry McCance, Geraldine Acuna-Sunshine, Craig McCaw, Susan McCaw, Tim Reynolds, Scott Heimlich, Eduardo Cetlin, Gisèle Huff, Jerry Hume, Darren Woods, Robert Bradway, Gary Wilson, Jeff and Tricia Raikes, Bobby Kotick, Mason and Logan Angel, Angela Duckworth, Ethan Mollick, Chris Anderson, and Francis Ford Coppola, for being incredible supporters, advisers, and mentors.

Greg Brockman, Sam Altman, and Jessica Shieh, for your partnership on this AI journey.

The entire Khan Academy team, including the individuals below who were instrumental in our early concepts and launch:

Engineering: Paul Morgan, Shawn Jansepar, Sujata Salem, Jason Chancey, Pepper Miller, Mark Sandstrom, Sean Driedger-Bauer, John Resig, Kelli Hill, Chase Carnaroli, Jason Voll, Jack Zhang, Hunter Liu, RJ Corwin, Salman Omer, Zachary Plummer, Alice

Pao, Jeanette Head, Brian Genisio, Jonathan Price, Liz Faubell, Mahtab Sabet, Robert Pippin, Sarah E.S. Proffitt, Walt Wells, Matthew Curtis, Ned Redmond, Nicole Watts, Rachel Roberts, Sarah Third, David Braley, Kathy Phillip, Luke Smith, Andrew Pagan, Alex Morelli, Maddy Andrade-Ozaette, Amos Latteier, Elise McCrorie, Divya Chandrasekar, Emily Janzer, Ian Powell, Adam Berkan, Adam Goforth, Patrick McGill, Matt Morgan, Boris Lau, Erik Helal, Michael Mendoza, Nathan Dobrowolski, Kevin Barabash, Gerardo Gonzalez, Gina Valderrama, Danielle Whyte, Tim McCabe, Craig Silverstein, Miguel Castillo, Reid Mitchell, Cat Yannish.

Product, content, and design: Kristen DiCerbo, Ricky Chandarana, Adrienne Hunter Wong, Dave Travis, Laurie LeDuc, Daniel De Angulo, Sarah Robertson, Gintas Bradunas, Tommy Day, Susan August, Elvira Valdez, Corey Kollbocker, Jess Hendel, Heather Meston, Charlie Auen, Jeff Dodds, Nick Kokkinis, Anya Bila, Jonah Goldsaito, Lan Borg, Karen Shapiro.

Thank you to Stacey Olson, Vicki Zubovic, Regina Ross, Julian Roberts, Rachel Boroditsky, Julia Cowles, Sandeep Bapna, Jeremy Schifeling, Jason Hovey, Ted Chen, Craig Silverstein, Diana Olin, Jordan Peavey, Evan Rahman, Eirene Chen, Barb Kunz, Felipe Escamilla, Jesse Ambrose, for supporting and leading key parts of our work.

Special thanks to visionary education leaders including Dr. Katie Jenner, Commissioner Frank Edelblut, Superintendent Peggy Buffington, Dr. Jose Fuentes, Alan Usherenko, Tim Nellegar, and all the remarkable educators and students at Newark Public Schools, School City of Hobart, and our partner districts in Indiana and across the country.

My thanks to Richard Pine, Eliza Rothstein, Inkwell Management, Ibrahim Ahmad, Lee Kravetz, Carolyn Coleburn, Yuleza Negron,

ACKNOWLEDGMENTS

Bridget Gilleran, Molly Fessenden, Barb Kunz, Elizabeth Pham Janowski, Alex Cruz-Jimenez, Carrie Cook, Suzanne Roberts, Tom Greene, Tomer Altman, Joanna Samuels, Roger Studley, Eric Berson, Mimi Kravetz.

Huge thanks to Jeremiah Hennessy for convincing me to quit my day job in 2009.

I'd like to thank the hundreds of thousands of people who have donated to make Khan Academy possible and the hundreds of millions of learners, parents, and teachers who have chosen to use Khan Academy to uplift themselves and those they care about.

Last, but not least, thank you benevolent aliens for helping us help prepare humanity for first contact. Onward!

Notes

PART I: RISE OF THE AI TUTOR

4 **"Today we are facing":** Jeremy Weissman, "ChatGPT Is a Plague upon Education," *Inside Higher Ed*, Feb. 9, 2023, www.insidehighered.com/views/2023/02/09/chatgpt-plague -upon-education-opinion.

PART II: GIVING VOICE TO THE SOCIAL SCIENCES

37 **Based on a 2020 Gallup analysis:** Jonathan Rothwell, "Assessing the Economic Gains of Eradicating Illiteracy Nationally and Regionally in the United States," Gallup, Sept. 8, 2020, www.barbarabush.org/wp-content/uploads/2020/09/BBFoundation_Gains FromEradicatingIlliteracy_9_8.pdf.

43 **"The human mind":** Noam Chomsky, Ian Roberts, and Jeffrey Watumull, "The False Promise of ChatGPT," *New York Times*, March 8, 2023, www.nytimes.com/2023/03/08 /opinion/noam-chomsky-chatgpt-ai.html.

58 **"I must admit":** Gillian Brockell, "We 'Interviewed' Harriet Tubman Using AI. It Got a Little Weird," *Washington Post*, July 14, 2023, www.washingtonpost.com/history/inter active/2023/harriet-tubman-articial-intelligence-khan-academy/.

PART III: EMPOWERING THE NEXT INNOVATORS

86 **Based on a 2015:** U.S. Department of Education Office for Civil Rights, 2015–16 Civil Rights Data Collection, "Stem Course Taking," April 2018, www2.ed.gov/about/offices /list/ocr/docs/stem-course-taking.pdf.

PART IV: BETTER TOGETHER

107 *Journal of Medical Internet Research*: Alaa Ali Abd-Alrazaq et al., "Effectiveness and Safety of Using Chatbots to Improve Mental Health: Systematic Review and Meta-analysis," *Journal of Medical Internet Research* 22, no. 7 (July 2020), doi:10.2196/16021.

PART V: KEEPING KIDS SAFE

121 **In an age where misinformation:** Philip N. Howard et al., "Digital Misinformation/ Disinformation and Children," UNICEF Office of Global Insight and Policy, Aug. 2021, www.unicef.org/globalinsight/media/2096/file/UNICEF-Global-Insight-Digital-Mis -Disinformation-and-Children-2021.pdf.

122 Most measures of mental health: Jon D. Elhai et al., "Problematic Smartphone Use: A Conceptual Overview and Systemic Review of Relations with Anxiety and Depression Psychopathology," *Journal of Affective Disorders* 207 (2017), www.sciencedirect.com /science/article/abs/pii/S0165032716303196?via%3Dihub.

123 Many of these things: Steven Pinker, "The Media Exaggerates Negative News. This Distortion Has Consequences," *Guardian*, Feb. 17, 2018, www.theguardian.com/commentisfree /2018/feb/17/steven-pinker-media-negative-news.

134 Child psychology research: Tom Huddleston Jr., "Ivy League Child Psychologist: Let Your Kid Use ChatGPT—But Only If You Do These 3 Things First," CNBC, July 20, 2023, https://www.cnbc.com/2023/07/29/ivy-league-child-psychologist-how-parents-can -help-kids-use-ai-safely.html.

PART VI: THE TEACHING IN THE AGE OF AI

148 49 percent of that time: Ileana Najarro, "Here's How Many Hours a Week Teachers Work," EducationWeek, April 14, 2022, https://www.edweek.org/teaching-learning /heres-how-many-hours-a-week-teachers-work/2022/04.

160 According to a 2021 *Inside Higher Ed*: Melissa Ezarik, "Shades of Gray on Student Cheating," *Inside Higher Ed*, December 6, 2021, https://www.insidehighered.com/news /2021/12/07/what-students-see-cheating-and-how-allegations-are-handled.

160 Another *Inside Higher Ed*: Johanna Alonso, "In Proctoring Debate, Stanford Faculty Takes 'Nuclear Option,'" *Inside Higher Ed*, May 5, 2023, https://www.insidehighered .com/news/students/academics/2023/05/05/proctoring-debate-stanford-faculty-takes -nuclear-option.

160 According to a 2023 survey: Ryan McElroy and Evan Weiss, "Zeitgeist 5.0," *The Middlebury Campus*, May 2023, https://www.middleburycampus.com/article/2023/05 /zeitgeist-5-0.

160 According to Debra Satz: Chelcey Adami, "Faculty Senate Approves Changes to Honor Code, Judicial Charter," *StanfordReport*, April 27, 2023, https://news.stanford .edu/report/2023/04/27/faculty-senate-approves-changes-honor-code-judicial-charter/.

161 *The New York Times* profiled: Farah Stockman and Carlos Mureithi, "Cheating, Inc.: How Writing Papers for American College Students Has Become a Lucrative Profession Overseas," *New York Times*, September 7, 2019, https://www.nytimes.com/2019/09/07 /us/college-cheating-papers.html.

PART VII: THE GLOBAL CLASSROOM

168 A 2004 UNESCO study: Nazmul Chaudhury et al., "Teacher Absence in India: A Snapshot," UNESCO's International Institute for Educational Planning, 2004, https://etico .iiep.unesco.org/en/teacher-absence-india-snapshot#:~:text=25%25%20of %20teachers%20were%20absent,concentrated%20in%20the%20poorer%20states.

PART VIII: AI, ASSESSMENTS, AND ADMISSIONS

181 "students who engaged": "Elevating Math Scores: The Ongoing Success of MAP Accelerator," Khan Academy, 2022, https://blog.khanacademy.org/wp-content/uploads/2023 /09/MAP_Accelerator_21_22_Brief-1.pdf.

194 Alumni interviewers gave: Anemona Hartocollis, "Harvard Rated Asian-American Applicants Lower on Personality Traits, Suit Says," *New York Times*, June 15, 2018, https:// www.nytimes.com/2018/06/15/us/harvard-asian-enrollment-applicants.html.

PART IX: WORK AND WHAT COMES NEXT

203 Early controlled studies: Michael Chui, "Forward Thinking on the Brave New World of Generative AI with Ethan Mollick," McKinsey Global Institute, May 31, 2023, www .mckinsey.com/mgi/forward-thinking/forward-thinking-on-the-brave-new-world -of-generative-ai-with-ethan-mollick.

Index

INDEX

INDEX

INDEX

knowledge gaps, 13–14, 149–50, 155, 167
  math, 81, 84
Krieg, Tim, 91–92
Kubrick, Stanley, 213
Kurzweil, Ray, 41
Kurzweil Reading Machine, 41–43

labor
  AI and specialization of, 204
  AI lifting skills of, 219
lack, of core courses, 86
language, of AI tutor, 19–20
language algorithm, xxvi
large language model, xvi–xviii, xxi, xxiii,
    xxxii, 5
  as facilitator, 98–99, 118
  fear and, 95
  image recognition by, 48
  influencing, 126–27
  multilingual abilities of, 175–76
  responding to pandemic, 173–74
  science and, 67–68
  subconscious brain activity compared to,
    44–45
  as teacher productivity tool, 78–79
  in the workplace, 6
launch
  of GPT-4, 10–11
  of Khanmigo, 10–11, 17–18
layoffs, due to AI, 197, 199
learning, 108
  active, 150
  collaborative, 95–99
  equal-opportunity, 167–69, 171
  mastery of, 15
  students as active participants in, 22
learning, one-on-one, xiii–xiv, 12–14
lesson plan
  baseball in, 152
  from generative AI, 151–53
letters, of recommendation, 186
  AI writing, 193
limitations
  of education access, 172–73, 175
  of traditional tutoring, 109
limited education resources, 172
literary characters, talking with, 36–37
Loeb, Susanna, 168–69, 170, 171, 176
logging off, 115–16
loneliness, 103
Los Angeles Unified School District, 3

marketplace, AI-infused, 197
mass media, misinformation and bias
  from, 123

mastery learning, 15
math gap, AI narrowing, 76–84
"A Mathematical Theory of Communication"
  (Shannon), xxi
meditation, 44–45
memory
  of AI tutor, 19–21
  of Khanmigo, 129–30
  power of, 11
mental health
  of adults, 138
  crisis in, 103
  intervention for, 105–7
  of students, 100–106
  of young people, 122
Middlebury College, 160
mimicking human behavior, xvi
Minsky, Marvin, 213
Miranda, Lin-Manuel, 62–63
misinformation and bias
  in AI, 121, 124–25
  in AI for college admissions, 193
  government reinforcing, 123
  in hiring process, 123–24
  on internet, 135
  in Khanmigo, 125–26
  in mass media, 123
  from social media, 121, 122, 123
  in standardized testing, 184
MIT, xxii
  Artificial Intelligence Laboratory, 102,
    212–13
  financial aid from, 214
models. *See also* large language model
  alternative education, 155–56, 157–58
  American education, 167
  language, xvi–xvii, xxi, xxiii, xxxii
  parameters of, xviii
  Pathways Language Model 2, 127
Mollick, Ethan, 32–33, 145–46, 147, 200, 203
Montgomery County, Alabama, 3
motivation and accountability, from tutor,
  88–89
multilingual abilities, of large language
  model, 175–76
multiple-choice questions, 38–39
  standardized tests using, 179, 183
Murthy, Vivek, 103

Nadia (cousin), xiii, 111
national security, generative AI and, 220
natural selection, AI-induced, 199
Nealey, Robert, xv
needs, of students and teachers, 90, 155
negative uses, of technology, 5

INDEX